MznLnx

Missing Links Exam Preps

Exam Prep for

Marketing Management

Peter & Donnelly, 9th Edition

The MznLnx Exam Prep is your link from the texbook and lecture to your exams.
The MznLnx Exam Preps are unauthorized and comprehensive reviews of your textbooks.

MznLnx

Rico
Publications

Exam Prep for Marketing Management
9th Edition
Peter & Donnelly

Publisher: Raymond Houge
Assistant Editor: Michael Rouger
Text and Cover Designer: Lisa Buckner
Marketing Manager: Sara Swagger
Project Manager, Editorial Production: Jerry Emerson
Art Director: Vernon Lowerui

Product Manager: Dave Mason
Editorial Assitant: Rachel Guzmanji
Pedagogy: Debra Long
Cover Image: Jim Reed/Getty Images
Text and Cover Printer: City Printing, Inc.
Compositor: Media Mix, Inc.

Printed in the United States
ISBN:

For more information about our products, contact us at:
Dave.Mason@RicoPublications.com

For permission to use material from this text or product, submit a request online to:
Dave.Mason@RicoPublications.com

Contents

TO THE STUDENT

COMPREHENSIVE

The *MznLnx* Exam Prep series is designed to help you pass your exams. Editors at MznLnx review your textbooks and then prepare these practice exams to help you master the textbook material. Unlike study guides, workbooks, and practice tests provided by the texbook publisher and textbook authors, *MznLnx* gives you ***all*** of the material in each chapter in exam form, not just samples, so you can be sure to nail your exam.

MECHANICAL

The MznLnx Exam Prep series creates exams that will help you learn the subject matter as well as test you on your understanding. Each question is designed to help you master the concept. Just working through the exams, you gain an understanding of the subject--its a simple mechanical process that produces success.

INTEGRATED STUDY GUIDE AND REVIEW

MznLnx is not just a set of exams designed to test you, its also a comprehensive review of the subject content. Each exam question is also a review of the concept, making sure that you will get the answer correct without having to go to other sources of material. You learn as you go! Its the easiest way to pass an exam.

HUMOR

Studying can be tedious and dry. MznLnx's instructional design includes moderate humor within the exam questions on occassion, to break the tedium and revitalize the brain

1. In economics, business, retail, and accounting, a _________ is the value of money that has been used up to produce something, and hence is not available for use anymore. In economics, a _________ is an alternative that is given up as a result of a decision. In business, the _________ may be one of acquisition, in which case the amount of money expended to acquire it is counted as _________.

a. Transaction cost | b. Fixed costs
c. Variable cost | d. Cost

2. The Oxford University Press defines _________ as 'marketing on a worldwide scale reconciling or taking commercial advantage of global operational differences, similarities and opportunities in order to meet global objectives.' Oxford University Press' Glossary of Marketing Terms.

Here are three reasons for the shift from domestic to _________ as given by the authors of the textbook, _________ Management--3rd Edition by Masaaki Kotabe and Kristiaan Helsen, 2004.

One of the product categories in which global competition has been easy to track is in U.S. automotive sales.

a. Guerrilla Marketing | b. Global marketing
c. Digital marketing | d. Diversity marketing

3. In economic models, the _________ time frame assumes no fixed factors of production. Firms can enter or leave the marketplace, and the cost (and availability) of land, labor, raw materials, and capital goods can be assumed to vary. In contrast, in the short-run time frame, certain factors are assumed to be fixed, because there is not sufficient time for them to change.

a. 6-3-5 Brainwriting | b. 180SearchAssistant
c. Power III | d. Long-run

4. _________ is defined by the American _________ Association as the activity, set of institutions, and processes for creating, communicating, delivering, and exchanging offerings that have value for customers, clients, partners, and society at large. The term developed from the original meaning which referred literally to going to market, as in shopping, or going to a market to sell goods or services.

_________ practice tends to be seen as a creative industry, which includes advertising, distribution and selling.

a. Marketing | b. Product naming
c. Marketing myopia | d. Customer acquisition management

5. _________ is an advertisement in which a particular product specifically mentions a competitor by name for the express purpose of showing why the competitor is inferior to the product naming it.

This should not be confused with parody advertisements, where a fictional product is being advertised for the purpose of poking fun at the particular advertisement, nor should it be confused with the use of a coined brand name for the purpose of comparing the product without actually naming an actual competitor. ('Wikipedia tastes better and is less filling than the Encyclopedia Galactica.')

In the 1980s, during what has been referred to as the cola wars, soft-drink manufacturer Pepsi ran a series of advertisements where people, caught on hidden camera, in a blind taste test, chose Pepsi over rival Coca-Cola.

a. Heavy-up
b. GL-70
c. Cost per conversion
d. Comparative advertising

6. The _________ is a professional association for marketers. As of 2008 it had approximately 40,000 members. There are collegiate chapters on 250 campuses.

a. ACNielsen
b. ADTECH
c. AMAX
d. American Marketing Association

7. _________ is a branch of philosophy which seeks to address questions about morality, such as how a moral outcome can be achieved in a specific situation (applied _________), how moral values should be determined (normative _________), what moral values people actually abide by (descriptive _________), what the fundamental semantic, ontological, and epistemic nature of _________ or morality is (meta-_________), and how moral capacity or moral agency develops and what its nature is (moral psychology.)

Socrates was one of the first Greek philosophers to encourage both scholars and the common citizen to turn their attention from the outside world to the condition of man. In this view, Knowledge having a bearing on human life was placed highest, all other knowledge being secondary.

a. ACNielsen
b. Ethics
c. AMAX
d. ADTECH

8. _________ or cause-related marketing refers to a type of marketing involving the cooperative efforts of a 'for profit' business and a non-profit organization for mutual benefit. The term is sometimes used more broadly and generally to refer to any type of marketing effort for social and other charitable causes, including in-house marketing efforts by non-profit organizations. _________ differs from corporate giving (philanthropy) as the latter generally involves a specific donation that is tax deductible, while _________ is a marketing relationship generally not based on a donation.

a. Cause-related Marketing
b. Global marketing
c. Cause marketing
d. Digital marketing

9. _________ deals with the first of the '4P''s of marketing, which are Product, Pricing, Place, and Promotion. _________, as opposed to product management, deals with more outbound marketing tasks. For example, product management deals with the nuts and bolts of product development within a firm, whereas _________ deals with marketing the product to prospects, customers, and others.

a. Product marketing
b. Corporate transparency
c. Reverse hierarchy
d. Crisis management

10. _________ is an organization's process of defining its strategy and making decisions on allocating its resources to pursue this strategy, including its capital and people. Various business analysis techniques can be used in _________, including SWOT analysis (Strengths, Weaknesses, Opportunities, and Threats) and PEST analysis (Political, Economic, Social, and Technological analysis) or STEER analysis involving Socio-cultural, Technological, Economic, Ecological, and Regulatory factors and EPISTEL (Environment, Political, Informatic, Social, Technological, Economic and Legal)

_________ is the formal consideration of an organization's future course. All _________ deals with at least one of three key questions:

1. 'What do we do?'
2. 'For whom do we do it?'
3. 'How do we excel?'

In business _________, the third question is better phrased 'How can we beat or avoid competition?'. (Bradford and Duncan, page 1.)

a. 6-3-5 Brainwriting
b. 180SearchAssistant
c. Power III
d. Strategic planning

11. _________ is a business discipline which is focused on the practical application of marketing techniques and the management of a firm's marketing resources and activities. Marketing managers are often responsible for influencing the level, timing, and composition of customer demand accepted definition of the term. In part, this is because the role of a marketing manager can vary significantly based on a business' size, corporate culture, and industry context.

a. Marketing management
b. Door-to-door
c. Performance-based advertising
d. Business structure

12. _________ in organizations and public policy is both the organizational process of creating and maintaining a plan; and the psychological process of thinking about the activities required to create a desired goal on some scale. As such, it is a fundamental property of intelligent behavior. This thought process is essential to the creation and refinement of a plan, or integration of it with other plans, that is, it combines forecasting of developments with the preparation of scenarios of how to react to them.

a. Planning
b. 180SearchAssistant
c. Power III
d. 6-3-5 Brainwriting

13. _________ is a broad label that refers to any individuals or households that use goods and services generated within the economy. The concept of a _________ is used in different contexts, so that the usage and significance of the term may vary.

A _________ is a person who uses any product or service.

a. 180SearchAssistant
b. Power III
c. 6-3-5 Brainwriting
d. Consumer

14. A _________ is a brief statement of the purpose of a company, organization. It is ideally used to guide the actions of the organization.

_________s often contain the following:

- Purpose of the organization
- The organization's primary stakeholders: clients, stockholders, etc.
- Responsibilities of the organization towards these stockholders
- Products and services offered

Generally shorter _________s are more effective than longer ones.

In developing a _________:

- Encourage input as feasible from employees, volunteers, and other stakeholders
- Publicize it broadly

The _________ can be used to resolve differences between business stakeholders. Stakeholders include: employees including managers and executives, stockholders, board of directors, customers, suppliers, distributors, creditors, governments (local, state, federal, etc.), unions, competitors, NGO's, and the general public.

a. 180SearchAssistant
b. Power III
c. 6-3-5 Brainwriting
d. Mission statement

15. A _________ is a plan of action designed to achieve a particular goal.

_________ is different from tactics. In military terms, tactics is concerned with the conduct of an engagement while _________ is concerned with how different engagements are linked.

a. Strategy
b. Power III
c. 6-3-5 Brainwriting
d. 180SearchAssistant

16. Levi Strauss, born Löb Strauss (February 26, 1829 - September 26, 1902) was a German-Jewish immigrant to the United States who founded the first company to manufacture blue jeans. His firm, _________, began in 1853 in San Francisco, California.

Levi Strauss was born in Bavaria, Germany, to Hirsch Strauss and his wife Rebecca (Haas) Strauss.

a. AStore
b. Levi Strauss ' Company
c. African Americans
d. Albert Einstein

17. _________ is the practice of individuals including commercial businesses, governments and institutions, facilitating the sale of their products or services to other companies or organizations that in turn resell them, use them as components in products or services they offer _________ is also called business-to-_________ for short. (Note that while marketing to government entities shares some of the same dynamics of organizational marketing, B2G Marketing is meaningfully different.)

a. Disruptive technology
b. Law of disruption
c. Mass marketing
d. Business marketing

18. Procter is a surname, and may also refer to:

- Bryan Waller Procter (pseud. Barry Cornwall), English poet
- Goodwin Procter, American law firm
- _________, consumer products multinational

.

a. Black PRies
b. Procter ' Gamble
c. Flyer
d. Convergent

19. _________ is the set of reasons that determines one to engage in a particular behavior. The term is generally used for human _________ but, theoretically, it can be used to describe the causes for animal behavior as well
a. 180SearchAssistant
b. Motivation
c. Role playing
d. Power III

20. _________ is a form of communication that typically attempts to persuade potential customers to purchase or to consume more of a particular brand of product or service. 'While now central to the contemporary global economy and the reproduction of global production networks, it is only quite recently that _________ has been more than a marginal influence on patterns of sales and production. The formation of modern _________ was intimately bound up with the emergence of new forms of monopoly capitalism around the end of the 19th and beginning of the 20th century as one element in corporate strategies to create, organize and where possible control markets, especially for mass produced consumer goods.
a. Advertising
b. AMAX
c. ACNielsen
d. ADTECH

21. In economics, an externality or spillover of an economic transaction is an impact on a party that is not directly involved in the transaction. In such a case, prices do not reflect the full costs or benefits in production or consumption of a product or service. A positive impact is called an _________ benefit, while a negative impact is called an _________ cost.
a. AMAX
b. ACNielsen
c. External
d. ADTECH

22. _________ is a measure of the strength of a brand, product, service relative to competitive offerings. There is often a geographic element to the competitive landscape. In defining _________, you must see to what extent a product, brand, or firm controls a product category in a given geographic area.
a. Market dominance
b. Productivity
c. Discretionary spending
d. Market system

23. _________ is one of the four growth strategies of the Product-Market Growth Matrix defined by Ansoff. _________ occurs when a company enters/penetrates a market with current products. The best way to achieve this is by gaining competitors' customers (part of their market share.)
a. Horizontal market
b. Marketization
c. Pasar pagi
d. Market penetration

24. The phrase _________, according to the Organization for Economic Co-operation and Development, refers to 'creative work undertaken on a systematic basis in order to increase the stock of knowledge, including knowledge of man, culture and society, and the use of this stock of knowledge to devise new applications [sic]' Though it is questionable that an organization is needed for this definition, as it is quite obvious that _________ refers to the _________ of something.

New product design and development is more often than not a crucial factor in the survival of a company. In an industry that is fast changing, firms must continually revise their design and range of products.

a. Power III
b. Research and development
c. 6-3-5 Brainwriting
d. 180SearchAssistant

25. _________ refers to the methods of practicing and using another person's philosophy of business. The franchisor grants the independent operator the right to distribute its products, techniques, and trademarks for a percentage of gross monthly sales and a royalty fee. Various tangibles and intangibles such as national or international advertising, training, and other support services are commonly made available by the franchisor.

a. Franchise fee
b. Power III
c. 180SearchAssistant
d. Franchising

26. Human beings are also considered to be _________ because they have the ability to change raw materials into valuable _________. The term Human _________ can also be defined as the skills, energies, talents, abilities and knowledge that are used for the production of goods or the rendering of services. While taking into account human beings as _________, the following things have to be kept in mind:

- The size of the population
- The capabilities of the individuals in that population

Many _________ cannot be consumed in their original form. They have to be processed in order to change them into more usable commodities.

a. 180SearchAssistant
b. 6-3-5 Brainwriting
c. Resources
d. Power III

27. Competitiveness is a comparative concept of the ability and performance of a firm, sub-sector or country to sell and supply goods and/or services in a given market. Although widely used in economics and business management, the usefulness of the concept, particularly in the context of national competitiveness, is vigorously disputed by economists, such as Paul Krugman .

The term may also be applied to markets, where it is used to refer to the extent to which the market structure may be regarded as perfectly _________.

a. Geographical pricing
b. Customs union
c. Free trade zone
d. Competitive

28. _________ is, in very basic words, a position a firm occupies against its competitors.

According to Michael Porter, the three methods for creating a sustainable _________ are through:

1. Cost leadership - Cost advantage occurs when a firm delivers the same services as its competitors but at a lower cost;

2.

a. 180SearchAssistant
b. 6-3-5 Brainwriting
c. Power III
d. Competitive advantage

29. A _________ strategy targets non-buying customers in currently targeted segments. It also targets new customers in new segments. (Winer)

A marketing manager has to think about the following questions before implementing a _________ strategy: Is it profitable? Will it require the introduction of new or modified products? Is the customer and channel well enough researched and understood?

The marketing manager uses these four groups to give more focus to the market segment decision: existing customers, competitor customers, non-buying in current segments, new segments.

a. Kano model
b. Market development
c. Commercial planning
d. Perceptual mapping

30. In business and engineering, new _________ is the term used to describe the complete process of bringing a new product or service to market. There are two parallel paths involved in the Nproduct development process: one involves the idea generation, product design, and detail engineering; the other involves market research and marketing analysis. Companies typically see new _________ as the first stage in generating and commercializing new products within the overall strategic process of product life cycle management used to maintain or grow their market share.

a. New product development
b. Specification tree
c. Product development
d. New product screening

31. _________ is a concept developed by Michael Porter, used in business strategy. It describes a way to establish the competitive advantage. _________, in basic words, means the lowest cost of operation in the industry.

a. Cost leadership
b. Chaotics
c. Strategic group
d. Corporate strategy

32. A _________ is a process that can allow an organization to concentrate its limited resources on the greatest opportunities to increase sales and achieve a sustainable competitive advantage. A _________ should be centered around the key concept that customer satisfaction is the main goal.

A _________ is most effective when it is an integral component of corporate strategy, defining how the organization will successfully engage customers, prospects, and competitors in the market arena.

a. Psychographic
b. Societal marketing
c. Cyberdoc
d. Marketing strategy

33. In marketing, _________ is the process of distinguishing the differences of a product or offering from others, to make it more attractive to a particular target market. This involves differentiating it from competitors' products as well as one's own product offerings.

Differentiation is a source of competitive advantage.

a. Marketing myopia
b. Corporate image
c. Packshot
d. Product differentiation

34.

Competitive advantage is, in very basic words, a position a firm occupies against its competitors. According to Michael Porter, the three methods for creating a _________ are through:

Cost leadership - Cost advantage occurs when a firm delivers the same services as its competitors but at a lower cost;

Differentiation - Differentiation advantage occurs when a firm delivers greater services for the same price of its competitors. They are collectively known as positional advantages because they denote the firm's position in its industry as a leader in either superior services or cost;

Focus (economics) - A focused approach requires the firm to concentrate on a narrow, exclusive competitive segment (market niche), hoping to achieve a local rather than industry wide competitive advantage. There are cost focus seekers, who aim to obtain a local cost advantage over competition and differentiation focuser, who are looking for a local difference.

a. 180SearchAssistant
b. 6-3-5 Brainwriting
c. Power III
d. Sustainable competitive advantage

35. A personal and cultural _________ is a relative ethic _________, an assumption upon which implementation can be extrapolated. A _________ system is a set of consistent _________s and measures that is soo not true. A principle _________ is a foundation upon which other _________s and measures of integrity are based.

a. Package-on-Package
b. Value
c. Supreme Court of the United States
d. Perceptual maps

36. _________ is understood as a business unit within the overall corporate identity which is distinguishable from other business because it serves a defined external market where management can conduct strategic planning in relation to products and markets. When companies become really large, they are best thought of as being composed of a number of businesses (or _________s.)

In the broader domain of strategic management, the phrase '_________' came into use in the 1960s, largely as a result of General Electric's many units.

a. Strategic business unit
b. Corporate strategy
c. Cost leadership
d. Business strategy

37. _________ is a marketing term, and involves evaluating the situation and trends in a particular company's market. _________ is often called the 'three c's', which refers to the three major elements that must be studied:

- Customers
- Costs
- Competition

The number of 'c's' is sometimes extended to four, five, or even six, with 'Collaboration', 'Company', and 'Competitive advantage'.

- Marketing mix
- SWOT analysis

.

a. Power III
b. Situation analysis
c. 6-3-5 Brainwriting
d. 180SearchAssistant

38. A _________ is defined by the International Co-operative Alliance's Statement on the Co-operative Identity as an autonomous association of persons united voluntarily to meet their common economic, social, and cultural needs and aspirations through a jointly-owned and democratically-controlled enterprise. It is a business organization owned and operated by a group of individuals for their mutual benefit. A _________ may also be defined as a business owned and controlled equally by the people who use its services or who work at it.

a. 180SearchAssistant
b. Cooperative
c. 6-3-5 Brainwriting
d. Power III

39. _________s is the social science that studies the production, distribution, and consumption of goods and services. The term _________s comes from the Ancient Greek oá¼°κονομÎ¯α from oá¼¶κος (oikos, 'house') + νÏŒμος (nomos, 'custom' or 'law'), hence 'rules of the house(hold)'. Current _________ models developed out of the broader field of political economy in the late 19th century, owing to a desire to use an empirical approach more akin to the physical sciences.

a. ADTECH
b. ACNielsen
c. Industrial organization
d. Economic

40. _________ refer to a collection of facts usually collected as the result of experience, observation or experiment or a set of premises. This may consist of numbers, words particularly as measurements or observations of a set of variables. _________ are often viewed as a lowest level of abstraction from which information and knowledge are derived.

a. Data
b. Pearson product-moment correlation coefficient
c. Sample size
d. Mean

41. _________ is a term used to describe a process of preparing and collecting data - for example as part of a process improvement or similar project.

_________ usually takes place early on in an improvement project, and is often formalised through a _________ Plan which often contains the following activity.

1. Pre collection activity - Agree goals, target data, definitions, methods
2. Collection - _________
3. Present Findings - usually involves some form of sorting analysis and/or presentation.

A formal _________ process is necessary as it ensures that data gathered is both defined and accurate and that subsequent decisions based on arguments embodied in the findings are valid . The process provides both a baseline from which to measure from and in certain cases a target on what to improve. Types of _________ 1-By mail questionnaires 2-By personal interview

- Six sigma
- Sampling (statistics)

.

a. 180SearchAssistant
b. Power III
c. 6-3-5 Brainwriting
d. Data collection

42. A _________ is a written document that details the necessary actions to achieve one or more marketing objectives. It can be for a product or service, a brand, or a product line. _________s cover between one and five years.

a. Prosumer
b. Disruptive technology
c. Marketing strategy
d. Marketing plan

43. _________ is the realization of an application idea, model, design, specification, standard, algorithm an _________ is a realization of a technical specification or algorithm as a program, software component, or other computer system. Many _________s may exist for a given specification or standard.

a. Implementation
b. AMAX
c. ACNielsen
d. ADTECH

44. The _________ is generally accepted as the use and specification of the four p's describing the strategic position of a product in the marketplace. One version of the origins of the _________ starts in 1948 when James Culliton said that a marketing decision should be a result of something similar to a recipe. This version continued in 1953 when Neil Borden, in his American Marketing Association presidential address, took the recipe idea one step further and coined the term 'Marketing-Mix'.

a. Power III
b. 6-3-5 Brainwriting
c. 180SearchAssistant
d. Marketing mix

45. A _________ is a group of employees from various functional areas of the organization - research, engineering, marketing, finance. human resources, and operations, for example - who are all focused on a specific objective and are responsible to work as a team to improve coordination and innovation across divisions and resolve mutual problems.

a. 180SearchAssistant
b. Power III
c. Job analysis
d. Cross-functional team

46. Consumer market research is a form of applied sociology that concentrates on understanding the behaviours, whims and preferences, of consumers in a market-based economy, and aims to understand the effects and comparative success of marketing campaigns. The field of consumer _________ as a statistical science was pioneered by Arthur Nielsen with the founding of the ACNielsen Company in 1923 .

Thus _________ is the systematic and objective identification, collection, analysis, and dissemination of information for the purpose of assisting management in decision making related to the identification and solution of problems and opportunities in marketing.

a. Marketing research
b. Focus group
c. Marketing research process
d. Logit analysis

47. In business, a _________ is a product or a business unit that generates unusually high profit margins: so high that it is responsible for a large amount of a company's operating profit. This profit far exceeds the amount necessary to maintain the _________ business, and the excess is used by the business for other purposes.

A firm is said to be acting as a _________ when its earnings per share (EPS) is equal to its dividends per share (DPS), or in other words, when a firm pays out 100% of its free cash flow (FCF) to its shareholders as dividends at the end of each accounting term.

a. Corporate transparency
b. Goal setting
c. Crisis management
d. Cash cow

48. An _________ is the manufacturing of a good or service within a category. Although _________ is a broad term for any kind of economic production, in economics and urban planning _________ is a synonym for the secondary sector, which is a type of economic activity involved in the manufacturing of raw materials into goods and products.

There are four key industrial economic sectors: the primary sector, largely raw material extraction industries such as mining and farming; the secondary sector, involving refining, construction, and manufacturing; the tertiary sector, which deals with services (such as law and medicine) and distribution of manufactured goods; and the quaternary sector, a relatively new type of knowledge _________ focusing on technological research, design and development such as computer programming, and biochemistry.

a. AMAX
b. ADTECH
c. ACNielsen
d. Industry

1. _________ is a broad label that refers to any individuals or households that use goods and services generated within the economy. The concept of a _________ is used in different contexts, so that the usage and significance of the term may vary.

A _________ is a person who uses any product or service.

a. 180SearchAssistant
b. 6-3-5 Brainwriting
c. Power III
d. Consumer

2. _________ can be regarded as an outcome of mental processes (cognitive process) leading to the selection of a course of action among several alternatives. Every _________ process produces a final choice. The output can be an action or an opinion of choice.

a. 180SearchAssistant
b. Power III
c. 6-3-5 Brainwriting
d. Decision making

3. _________ is defined by the American _________ Association as the activity, set of institutions, and processes for creating, communicating, delivering, and exchanging offerings that have value for customers, clients, partners, and society at large. The term developed from the original meaning which referred literally to going to market, as in shopping, or going to a market to sell goods or services.

_________ practice tends to be seen as a creative industry, which includes advertising, distribution and selling.

a. Customer acquisition management
b. Product naming
c. Marketing myopia
d. Marketing

4. Consumer market research is a form of applied sociology that concentrates on understanding the behaviours, whims and preferences, of consumers in a market-based economy, and aims to understand the effects and comparative success of marketing campaigns. The field of consumer _________ as a statistical science was pioneered by Arthur Nielsen with the founding of the ACNielsen Company in 1923 .

Thus _________ is the systematic and objective identification, collection, analysis, and dissemination of information for the purpose of assisting management in decision making related to the identification and solution of problems and opportunities in marketing.

a. Logit analysis
b. Marketing research
c. Focus group
d. Marketing research process

5. _________ is a set of six steps which defines the tasks to be accomplished in conducting a marketing research study. These include problem definition, developing an approach to problem, research design formulation, field work, data preparation and analysis, and report generation and presentation.

a. Preference-rank translation
b. Market analysis
c. Simple random sampling
d. Marketing research process

6. _________ refer to a collection of facts usually collected as the result of experience, observation or experiment or a set of premises. This may consist of numbers, words particularly as measurements or observations of a set of variables. _________ are often viewed as a lowest level of abstraction from which information and knowledge are derived.

a. Pearson product-moment correlation coefficient
b. Mean
c. Sample size
d. Data

7. _________ is a term used to describe a process of preparing and collecting data - for example as part of a process improvement or similar project.

_________ usually takes place early on in an improvement project, and is often formalised through a _________ Plan which often contains the following activity.

1. Pre collection activity - Agree goals, target data, definitions, methods
2. Collection - _________
3. Present Findings - usually involves some form of sorting analysis and/or presentation.

A formal _________ process is necessary as it ensures that data gathered is both defined and accurate and that subsequent decisions based on arguments embodied in the findings are valid . The process provides both a baseline from which to measure from and in certain cases a target on what to improve. Types of _________ 1-By mail questionnaires 2-By personal interview

- Six sigma
- Sampling (statistics)

.

a. Data collection
b. 6-3-5 Brainwriting
c. Power III
d. 180SearchAssistant

8. A _________ is a form of qualitative research in which a group of people are asked about their attitude towards a product, service, concept, advertisement, idea, or packaging. Questions are asked in an interactive group setting where participants are free to talk with other group members.

Ernest Dichter originated the idea of having a 'group therapy' for products and this process is what became known as a _________.

a. Marketing research process
b. Focus group
c. Cross tabulation
d. Logit analysis

9. In marketing and the social sciences, _________ is a social research technique that involves the direct observation of phenomena in their natural setting. This differentiates it from experimental research in which a quasi-artificial environment is created to control for spurious factors, and where at least one of the variables is manipulated as part of the experiment.

Compared with quantitative research and experimental research, _________ tends to be less reliable but often more valid.

a. ADTECH
b. ACNielsen
c. AMAX
d. Observational research

10. _________ is a term for unprocessed data, it is also known as primary data. It is a relative term _________ can be input to a computer program or used in manual analysis procedures such as gathering statistics from a survey.

a. Raw data
b. Chief marketing officer
c. Product manager
d. Shoppers Food ' Pharmacy

11. A _________ attribute is one that exists in a range of magnitudes, and can therefore be measured. Measurements of any particular _________ property are expressed as a specific quantity, referred to as a unit, multiplied by a number. Examples of physical quantities are distance, mass, and time.

a. BeyondROI
b. Quantitative
c. Lifestyle city
d. Dolly Dimples

12. Combining Existing _________ Sources with New Primary Data Sources

Imagine that we could get hold of a good collection of surveys taken in earlier years, such as detailed studies about changes going on in this phase and hopefully additional studies in the years to come. Analyzing this data base over time could give us a good picture of what changes actually have taken place in the orientation of the population and of the extent to which new technical concepts did have an impact on subgroups of the population. Furthermore, data archives can help to prepare studies on change over time by monitoring what questions have been asked in earlier years and alerting principal investigators to important questions which should be repeated in planned research projects.

a. Power III
b. Secondary data
c. 6-3-5 Brainwriting
d. 180SearchAssistant

13. The _________ is a publication of the United States Census Bureau, an agency of the United States Department of Commerce. Published annually since 1878, the statistics describe social and economic conditions in the United States.

In 1975 a two volume Historical Statistics of the United States, Colonial Times to 1970 Bicentennial Edition was published.

a. Power III
b. Statistical Abstract of the United States
c. 180SearchAssistant
d. 6-3-5 Brainwriting

14. _________ a research method involving the use of questionnaires and/or statistical surveys to gather data about people and their thoughts and behaviours.

a. Control chart
b. T-test
c. Z-test
d. Survey research

15. _________ is either an activity of a living being (such as a human), consisting of receiving knowledge of the outside world through the senses, or the recording of data using scientific instruments. The term may also refer to any datum collected during this activity.

The scientific method requires _________s of nature to formulate and test hypotheses.

a. ADTECH
b. ACNielsen
c. Observation
d. AMAX

16. _________ is a global marketing research firm, with worldwide headquarters in New York City. Regional headquarters for North America are located in Schaumburg, IL. As of 2008, its the part of The Nielsen Company.

a. InfoNU
b. Alloy Entertainment
c. ACNielsen
d. E-Detailing

17. _________ is a radio audience research company in the United States which collects listener data on radio audiences similar to that collected by Nielsen Media Research on television audiences. It was founded as American Research Bureau by Jim Seiler in 1949 and became bi-coastal by merging with L.A. based Coffin, Cooper and Clay in the early 1950s. ARB's initial business was the collection of television broadcast ratings exclusively.

a. American Heart Association
b. Access Commerce
c. Arbitron
d. American Cancer Society

18. _________ is an American firm that measures media audiences, including television, radio, theatre films (via the AMC MAP program) and newspapers. _________, headquartered in New York City and operating primarily from Chicago, is best-known for the Nielsen Ratings, a measurement of television viewership.

_________, the preeminent media research company in the world, began as a division of ACNielsen, a marketing research firm.

a. Hennes ' Mauritz
b. CoolBrands
c. Nielsen Media Research
d. Green Earth Market

19. Human beings are also considered to be _________ because they have the ability to change raw materials into valuable _________. The term Human _________ can also be defined as the skills, energies, talents, abilities and knowledge that are used for the production of goods or the rendering of services. While taking into account human beings as _________, the following things have to be kept in mind:

- The size of the population
- The capabilities of the individuals in that population

Many _________ cannot be consumed in their original form. They have to be processed in order to change them into more usable commodities.

a. Resources
b. Power III
c. 180SearchAssistant
d. 6-3-5 Brainwriting

20. A _________ is a collection of symbols, experiences and associations connected with a product, a service, a person or any other artifact or entity.

_________s have become increasingly important components of culture and the economy, now being described as 'cultural accessories and personal philosophies'.

Some people distinguish the psychological aspect of a _________ from the experiential aspect.

a. Store brand
b. Brand
c. Brand equity
d. Brandable software

21. An _________ is the manufacturing of a good or service within a category. Although _________ is a broad term for any kind of economic production, in economics and urban planning _________ is a synonym for the secondary sector, which is a type of economic activity involved in the manufacturing of raw materials into goods and products.

There are four key industrial economic sectors: the primary sector, largely raw material extraction industries such as mining and farming; the secondary sector, involving refining, construction, and manufacturing; the tertiary sector, which deals with services (such as law and medicine) and distribution of manufactured goods; and the quaternary sector, a relatively new type of knowledge _________ focusing on technological research, design and development such as computer programming, and biochemistry.

a. ACNielsen
b. ADTECH
c. AMAX
d. Industry

22. In economics, _________ is the desire to own something and the ability to pay for it. The term _________ signifies the ability or the willingness to buy a particular commodity at a given point of time .

.

a. Market system
b. Market dominance
c. Discretionary spending
d. Demand

23. _________ in economics and business is the result of an exchange and from that trade we assign a numerical monetary value to a good, service or asset. If I trade 4 apples for an orange, the _________ of an orange is 4 - apples. Inversely, the _________ of an apple is 1/4 oranges.

a. Contribution margin-based pricing
b. Price
c. Discounts and allowances
d. Pricing

24. A _________ is a written document that details the necessary actions to achieve one or more marketing objectives. It can be for a product or service, a brand, or a product line. _________s cover between one and five years.

a. Disruptive technology
b. Marketing strategy
c. Marketing plan
d. Prosumer

25. _________ is the study of when, why, how, where and what people do or do not buy products. It blends elements from psychology, sociology,social psychology, anthropology and economics. It attempts to understand the buyer decision making process, both individually and in groups. It studies characteristics of individual consumers such as demographics and behavioural variables in an attempt to understand people's wants. It also tries to assess influences on the consumer from groups such as family, friends, reference groups, and society in general.

a. Consumer behavior
b. Multidimensional scaling
c. Communal marketing
d. Consumer confidence

26. _________ is the process of extracting hidden patterns from data. As more data is gathered, with the amount of data doubling every three years, _________ is becoming an increasingly important tool to transform this data into information. It is commonly used in a wide range of profiling practices, such as marketing, surveillance, fraud detection and scientific discovery.

a. Data mining
b. 180SearchAssistant
c. Structure mining
d. Power III

27. A _________, in the field of business and marketing, is a geographic region or demographic group used to gauge the viability of a product or service in the mass market prior to a wide scale roll-out. The criteria used to judge the acceptability of a _________ region or group include:

1. a population that is demographically similar to the proposed target market; and
2. relative isolation from densely populated media markets so that advertising to the test audience can be efficient and economical.

The _________ ideally aims to duplicate 'everything' - promotion and distribution as well as `product' - on a smaller scale. The technique replicates, typically in one area, what is planned to occur in a national launch; and the results are very carefully monitored, so that they can be extrapolated to projected national results. The `area' may be any one of the following:

- Television area
- Test town
- Residential neighborhood
- Test site

A number of decisions have to be taken about any _________:

- Which _________?
- What is to be tested?
- How long a test?
- What are the success criteria?

The simple go or no-go decision, together with the related reduction of risk, is normally the main justification for the expense of _________s. At the same time, however, such _________s can be used to test specific elements of a new product's marketing mix; possibly the version of the product itself, the promotional message and media spend, the distribution channels and the price.

a. Test market
b. Power III
c. Preadolescence
d. 180SearchAssistant

28. Wholesaling, historically called jobbing, is the sale of goods or merchandise to retailers, to industrial, commercial, institutional or to other wholesalers and related subordinated services.

According to the United Nations Statistics Division, '_________' is the resale (sale without transformation) of new and used goods to retailers, to industrial, commercial, institutional or professional users or involves acting as an agent or broker in buying merchandise for such persons or companies. Wholesalers frequently physically assemble, sort and grade goods in large lots, break bulk, repack and redistribute in smaller lots.

a. Supply network
b. Purchasing
c. Wholesale
d. Supply chain network

29. _________ is a form of communication that typically attempts to persuade potential customers to purchase or to consume more of a particular brand of product or service. 'While now central to the contemporary global economy and the reproduction of global production networks, it is only quite recently that _________ has been more than a marginal influence on patterns of sales and production. The formation of modern _________ was intimately bound up with the emergence of new forms of monopoly capitalism around the end of the 19th and beginning of the 20th century as one element in corporate strategies to create, organize and where possible control markets, especially for mass produced consumer goods.

a. AMAX
b. ADTECH
c. ACNielsen
d. Advertising

30. _________ generally refers to a list of all planned expenses and revenues. It is a plan for saving and spending. A _________ is an important concept in microeconomics, which uses a _________ line to illustrate the trade-offs between two or more goods.

a. Budget
b. 6-3-5 Brainwriting
c. Power III
d. 180SearchAssistant

31. _________ has been defined by the International Organization for Standardization (ISO) as 'ensuring that information is accessible only to those authorized to have access' and is one of the cornerstones of information security. _________ is one of the design goals for many cryptosystems, made possible in practice by the techniques of modern cryptography.

_________ also refers to an ethical principle associated with several professions (e.g., medicine, law, religion, professional psychology, and journalism.)

a. 6-3-5 Brainwriting
b. 180SearchAssistant
c. Power III
d. Confidentiality

32. A _________ is a group of employees from various functional areas of the organization - research, engineering, marketing, finance. human resources, and operations, for example - who are all focused on a specific objective and are responsible to work as a team to improve coordination and innovation across divisions and resolve mutual problems.

a. 180SearchAssistant
b. Cross-functional team
c. Power III
d. Job analysis

33. _________ is a branch of philosophy which seeks to address questions about morality, such as how a moral outcome can be achieved in a specific situation (applied _________), how moral values should be determined (normative _________), what moral values people actually abide by (descriptive _________), what the fundamental semantic, ontological, and epistemic nature of _________ or morality is (meta-_________), and how moral capacity or moral agency develops and what its nature is (moral psychology.)

Socrates was one of the first Greek philosophers to encourage both scholars and the common citizen to turn their attention from the outside world to the condition of man. In this view, Knowledge having a bearing on human life was placed highest, all other knowledge being secondary.

a. AMAX
b. Ethics
c. ACNielsen
d. ADTECH

34. _________ is a contract between two parties, one being the employer and the other being the employee. An employee may be defined as: 'A person in the service of another under any contract of hire, express or implied, oral or written, where the employer has the power or right to control and direct the employee in the material details of how the work is to be performed.' Black's Law Dictionary page 471 (5th ed. 1979.)

a. AMAX
b. Employment
c. ACNielsen
d. ADTECH

35. A _________ is a process that can allow an organization to concentrate its limited resources on the greatest opportunities to increase sales and achieve a sustainable competitive advantage. A _________ should be centered around the key concept that customer satisfaction is the main goal.

A _________ is most effective when it is an integral component of corporate strategy, defining how the organization will successfully engage customers, prospects, and competitors in the market arena.

a. Societal marketing
b. Cyberdoc
c. Psychographic
d. Marketing strategy

36. In economics, an externality or spillover of an economic transaction is an impact on a party that is not directly involved in the transaction. In such a case, prices do not reflect the full costs or benefits in production or consumption of a product or service. A positive impact is called an _________ benefit, while a negative impact is called an _________ cost.

a. ADTECH
b. ACNielsen
c. AMAX
d. External

37. _________ is an information system that helps with decision-making in the formation of a marketing plan. The reason for using an MKDSS is because it helps to support the software vendors' planning strategy for marketing products; it can help to identify advantageous levels of pricing, advertising spending, and advertising copy for the firm's products (Arinze, 1990.) This helps determines the firms marketing mix for product software.

a. 6-3-5 Brainwriting
b. Power III
c. 180SearchAssistant
d. Marketing decision support systems

38. _________ constitute a class of computer-based information systems including knowledge-based systems that support decision-making activities.

_________ are a specific class of computerized information system that supports business and organizational decision-making activities. A properly-designed _________ is an interactive software-based system intended to help decision makers compile useful information from raw data, documents, personal knowledge, and/or business models to identify and solve problems and make decisions.

a. Decision support systems
b. Power III
c. 180SearchAssistant
d. 6-3-5 Brainwriting

1. _________ is a broad label that refers to any individuals or households that use goods and services generated within the economy. The concept of a _________ is used in different contexts, so that the usage and significance of the term may vary.

A _________ is a person who uses any product or service.

a. Power III
b. Consumer
c. 6-3-5 Brainwriting
d. 180SearchAssistant

2. _________ is the study of when, why, how, where and what people do or do not buy products. It blends elements from psychology, sociology,social psychology, anthropology and economics. It attempts to understand the buyer decision making process, both individually and in groups. It studies characteristics of individual consumers such as demographics and behavioural variables in an attempt to understand people's wants. It also tries to assess influences on the consumer from groups such as family, friends, reference groups, and society in general.

a. Multidimensional scaling
b. Consumer confidence
c. Communal marketing
d. Consumer behavior

3. _________ is defined by the American _________ Association as the activity, set of institutions, and processes for creating, communicating, delivering, and exchanging offerings that have value for customers, clients, partners, and society at large. The term developed from the original meaning which referred literally to going to market, as in shopping, or going to a market to sell goods or services.

_________ practice tends to be seen as a creative industry, which includes advertising, distribution and selling.

a. Marketing
b. Marketing myopia
c. Product naming
d. Customer acquisition management

4. _________ is difficult to define. For example, in 1952, Alfred Kroeber and Clyde Kluckhohn compiled a list of 164 definitions of '_________' in _________: A Critical Review of Concepts and Definitions. However, the word '_________' is most commonly used in three basic senses:

- excellence of taste in the fine arts and humanities
- an integrated pattern of human knowledge, belief, and behavior that depends upon the capacity for symbolic thought and social learning
- the set of shared attitudes, values, goals, and practices that characterizes an institution, organization or group.

When the concept first emerged in eighteenth- and nineteenth-century Europe, it connoted a process of cultivation or improvement, as in agriculture or horticulture. In the nineteenth century, it came to refer first to the betterment or refinement of the individual, especially through education, and then to the fulfillment of national aspirations or ideals.

a. Culture
b. Albert Einstein
c. AStore
d. African Americans

5. In economics, an externality or spillover of an economic transaction is an impact on a party that is not directly involved in the transaction. In such a case, prices do not reflect the full costs or benefits in production or consumption of a product or service. A positive impact is called an _________ benefit, while a negative impact is called an _________ cost.

a. ADTECH
b. ACNielsen
c. AMAX
d. External

6. A personal and cultural _________ is a relative ethic _________, an assumption upon which implementation can be extrapolated. A _________ system is a set of consistent _________s and measures that is soo not true. A principle _________ is a foundation upon which other _________s and measures of integrity are based.

a. Supreme Court of the United States
b. Perceptual maps
c. Value
d. Package-on-Package

7. _________ can be regarded as an outcome of mental processes (cognitive process) leading to the selection of a course of action among several alternatives. Every _________ process produces a final choice. The output can be an action or an opinion of choice.

a. 6-3-5 Brainwriting
b. 180SearchAssistant
c. Power III
d. Decision making

8. _________ is systematic determination of merit, worth, and significance of something or someone using criteria against a set of standards. _________ often is used to characterize and appraise subjects of interest in a wide range of human enterprises, including the arts, criminal justice, foundations and non-profit organizations, government, health care, and other human services.

Depending on the topic of interest, there are professional groups which look to the quality and rigor of the _________ process.

a. AMAX
b. ACNielsen
c. ADTECH
d. Evaluation

9. In sociology, anthropology and cultural studies, a _________ is a group of people with a culture (whether distinct or hidden) which differentiates them from the larger culture to which they belong. If a particular _________ is characterized by a systematic opposition to the dominant culture, it may be described as a counterculture. As Ken Gelder notes, _________s are social, with their own shared conventions, values and rituals, but they can also seem 'immersed' or self-absorbed--another feature that distinguishes them from countercultures.

a. 6-3-5 Brainwriting
b. 180SearchAssistant
c. Subculture
d. Power III

10. _________ is a term used to describe a person who was born during the demographic Post-World War II baby boom. Many analysts now believe that two distinct cultural generations were born during this baby boom; the older generation is often called the Baby Boom Generation and the younger generation is often called Generation Jones. The term '_________' is sometimes used in a cultural context, and sometimes used to describe someone who was born during the post-WWII baby boom.

a. Greatest Generation
b. AStore
c. Baby boomer
d. Generation X

11. _________ in economics and business is the result of an exchange and from that trade we assign a numerical monetary value to a good, service or asset. If I trade 4 apples for an orange, the _________ of an orange is 4 - apples. Inversely, the _________ of an apple is 1/4 oranges.

a. Contribution margin-based pricing
b. Pricing
c. Discounts and allowances
d. Price

12. A _________ is a sociological concept referring to a group to which an individual or another group is compared.

_________s are used in order to evaluate and determine the nature of a given individual or other group's characteristics and sociological attributes. It is the group to which the individual relates or aspires relate himself or self psychologically.

a. Mociology
b. Minority
c. Power III
d. Reference group

13. A _________ is a collection of symbols, experiences and associations connected with a product, a service, a person or any other artifact or entity.

_________s have become increasingly important components of culture and the economy, now being described as 'cultural accessories and personal philosophies'.

Some people distinguish the psychological aspect of a _________ from the experiential aspect.

a. Store brand
b. Brand
c. Brand equity
d. Brandable software

14. _________ refers to the marketing effects or outcomes that accrue to a product with its brand name compared with those that would accrue if the same product did not have the brand name . And, at the root of these marketing effects is consumers' knowledge. In other words, consumers' knowledge about a brand makes manufacturers/advertisers respond differently or adopt appropriately adapt measures for the marketing of the brand .

a. Brand image
b. Brand equity
c. Product extension
d. Brand aversion

15. _________ is one of the four elements of marketing mix. An organization or set of organizations (go-betweens) involved in the process of making a product or service available for use or consumption by a consumer or business user.

The other three parts of the marketing mix are product, pricing, and promotion.

a. Comparison-Shopping agent
b. Japan Advertising Photographers' Association
c. Better Living Through Chemistry
d. Distribution

16. _________ refers to messages and related media used to communicate with a market. Those who practice advertising, branding, direct marketing, graphic design, marketing, packaging, promotion, publicity, sponsorship, public relations, sales, sales promotion and online marketing are termed marketing communicators, _________ managers, or more briefly as marcom managers.

a. Marketing communication
b. Merchandise
c. Sales promotion
d. Merchandising

17. _________ involves disseminating information about a product, product line, brand, or company. It is one of the four key aspects of the marketing mix. (The other three elements are product marketing, pricing, and distribution). P>_________ is generally sub-divided into two parts:

- Above the line _________: Promotion in the media (e.g. TV, radio, newspapers, Internet and Mobile Phones) in which the advertiser pays an advertising agency to place the ad
- Below the line _________: All other _________. Much of this is intended to be subtle enough for the consumer to be unaware that _________ is taking place. E.g. sponsorship, product placement, endorsements, sales _________, merchandising, direct mail, personal selling, public relations, trade shows

a. Bottling lines
b. Davie Brown Index
c. Promotion
d. Cashmere Agency

18. A _________ is a systematic approach to selling a product or service. A growing body of published literature approaches the _________ from the point of view of an engineering discipline

Reasons for having a well thought-out _________ include seller and buyer risk management, standardized customer interaction in sales, and scalable revenue generation.

a. Sales management
b. Request for proposal
c. Lead generation
d. Sales process

19. _________ refers to a business or organization attempting to acquire goods or services to accomplish the goals of the enterprise. Though there are several organizations that attempt to set standards in the _________ process, processes can vary greatly between organizations. Typically the word '_________' is not used interchangeably with the word 'procurement', since procurement typically includes Expediting, Supplier Quality, and Traffic and Logistics (T'L) in addition to _________.

a. Drop shipping
b. Supply network
c. Purchasing
d. Supply chain

20. Maslow's _________ is a theory in psychology, proposed by Abraham Maslow in his 1943 paper A Theory of Human Motivation, which he subsequently extended to include his observations of humans' innate curiosity.

Maslow studied what he called exemplary people such as Albert Einstein, Jane Addams, Eleanor Roosevelt, and Frederick Douglass rather than mentally ill or neurotic people, writing that 'the study of crippled, stunted, immature, and unhealthy specimens can yield only a cripple psychology and a cripple philosophy.' Maslow also studied the healthiest one percent of the college student population. In his book, The Farther Reaches of Human Nature, Maslow writes, 'By ordinary standards of this kind of laboratory research...

a. 6-3-5 Brainwriting
b. Power III
c. Hierarchy of needs
d. 180SearchAssistant

21. The Oxford University Press defines _________ as 'marketing on a worldwide scale reconciling or taking commercial advantage of global operational differences, similarities and opportunities in order to meet global objectives.' Oxford University Press' Glossary of Marketing Terms.

Here are three reasons for the shift from domestic to _________ as given by the authors of the textbook, _________ Management--3rd Edition by Masaaki Kotabe and Kristiaan Helsen, 2004.

One of the product categories in which global competition has been easy to track is in U.S. automotive sales.

a. Guerrilla Marketing
b. Diversity marketing
c. Global marketing
d. Digital marketing

22. _________ is a term that has been used in various psychology theories, often in slightly different ways (e.g., Goldstein, Maslow, Rogers.) The term was originally introduced by the organismic theorist Kurt Goldstein for the motive to realise all of one's potentialities. In his view, it is the master motive--indeed, the only real motive a person has, all others being merely manifestations of it.

a. Power III
b. 6-3-5 Brainwriting
c. 180SearchAssistant
d. Self-actualization

23. _________ is an advertisement in which a particular product specifically mentions a competitor by name for the express purpose of showing why the competitor is inferior to the product naming it.

This should not be confused with parody advertisements, where a fictional product is being advertised for the purpose of poking fun at the particular advertisement, nor should it be confused with the use of a coined brand name for the purpose of comparing the product without actually naming an actual competitor. ('Wikipedia tastes better and is less filling than the Encyclopedia Galactica.')

In the 1980s, during what has been referred to as the cola wars, soft-drink manufacturer Pepsi ran a series of advertisements where people, caught on hidden camera, in a blind taste test, chose Pepsi over rival Coca-Cola.

a. Comparative advertising
b. Heavy-up
c. Cost per conversion
d. GL-70

24. The _________ is a professional association for marketers. As of 2008 it had approximately 40,000 members. There are collegiate chapters on 250 campuses.

a. American Marketing Association
b. ACNielsen
c. AMAX
d. ADTECH

25. _________ is a branch of philosophy which seeks to address questions about morality, such as how a moral outcome can be achieved in a specific situation (applied _________), how moral values should be determined (normative _________), what moral values people actually abide by (descriptive _________), what the fundamental semantic, ontological, and epistemic nature of _________ or morality is (meta-_________), and how moral capacity or moral agency develops and what its nature is (moral psychology.)

Socrates was one of the first Greek philosophers to encourage both scholars and the common citizen to turn their attention from the outside world to the condition of man. In this view, Knowledge having a bearing on human life was placed highest, all other knowledge being secondary.

a. ADTECH b. Ethics
c. AMAX d. ACNielsen

26. _________ is one of the four Ps of the marketing mix. The other three aspects are product, promotion, and place. It is also a key variable in microeconomic price allocation theory.

a. Relationship based pricing b. Price
c. Pricing d. Competitor indexing

27. Cognition is the scientific term for 'the process of thought.' Its usage varies in different ways in accord with different disciplines: For example, in psychology and _________ science it refers to an information processing view of an individual's psychological functions. Other interpretations of the meaning of cognition link it to the development of concepts; individual minds, groups, organizations, and even larger coalitions of entities, can be modelled as 'societies' (Society of Mind), which cooperate to form concepts.

The autonomous elements of each 'society' would have the opportunity to demonstrate emergent behavior in the face of some crisis or opportunity.

a. Power III b. 180SearchAssistant
c. 6-3-5 Brainwriting d. Cognitive

28. _________ is an uncomfortable feeling caused by holding two contradictory ideas simultaneously. The 'ideas' or 'cognitions' in question may include attitudes and beliefs, and also the awareness of one's behavior. The theory of _________ proposes that people have a motivational drive to reduce dissonance by changing their attitudes, beliefs, and behaviors, or by justifying or rationalizing their attitudes, beliefs, and behaviors.

a. Power III b. 180SearchAssistant
c. Cognitive dissonance d. Perception

29. _________ is the subjective judgment that people make about the characteristics and severity of a risk. The phrase is most commonly used in reference to natural hazards and threats to the environment or health, such as nuclear power. Several theories have been proposed to explain why different people make different estimates of the dangerousness of risks.

a. 6-3-5 Brainwriting b. 180SearchAssistant
c. Power III d. Risk perception

30. _________ is a concept that denotes the precise probability of specific eventualities. Technically, the notion of _________ is independent from the notion of value and, as such, eventualities may have both beneficial and adverse consequences. However, in general usage the convention is to focus only on potential negative impact to some characteristic of value that may arise from a future event.

a. 180SearchAssistant b. Power III
c. 6-3-5 Brainwriting d. Risk

1. _________ is a term commonly used to describe commerce transactions between businesses like the one between a manufacturer and a wholesaler or a wholesaler and a retailer i.e both the buyer and the seller are business entity.This is unlike business-to-consumers (B2C) which involve a business entity and end consumer, or business-to-government (B2G) which involve a business entity and government.

The volume of B2B transactions is much higher than the volume of B2C transactions. The primary reason for this is that in a typical supply chain there will be many B2B transactions involving subcomponent or raw materials, and only one B2C transaction, specifically sale of the finished product to the end customer.

a. Business-to-business
b. Customer relationship management
c. Social marketing
d. Disruptive technology

2. An _________ is the manufacturing of a good or service within a category. Although _________ is a broad term for any kind of economic production, in economics and urban planning _________ is a synonym for the secondary sector, which is a type of economic activity involved in the manufacturing of raw materials into goods and products.

There are four key industrial economic sectors: the primary sector, largely raw material extraction industries such as mining and farming; the secondary sector, involving refining, construction, and manufacturing; the tertiary sector, which deals with services (such as law and medicine) and distribution of manufactured goods; and the quaternary sector, a relatively new type of knowledge _________ focusing on technological research, design and development such as computer programming, and biochemistry.

a. ADTECH
b. ACNielsen
c. AMAX
d. Industry

3. _________ is defined by the American _________ Association as the activity, set of institutions, and processes for creating, communicating, delivering, and exchanging offerings that have value for customers, clients, partners, and society at large. The term developed from the original meaning which referred literally to going to market, as in shopping, or going to a market to sell goods or services.

_________ practice tends to be seen as a creative industry, which includes advertising, distribution and selling.

a. Marketing myopia
b. Customer acquisition management
c. Product naming
d. Marketing

4. The _________ or _________ is used by business and government to classify and measure economic activity in Canada, Mexico and the United States. It has largely replaced the older Standard Industrial Classification system; however, certain government departments and agencies, such as the U.S. Securities and Exchange Commission (SEC), still use the SIC codes.

The _________ numbering system is a six-digit code.

a. 180SearchAssistant
b. Power III
c. 6-3-5 Brainwriting
d. North American Industry Classification System

5. _________ in organizations and public policy is both the organizational process of creating and maintaining a plan; and the psychological process of thinking about the activities required to create a desired goal on some scale. As such, it is a fundamental property of intelligent behavior. This thought process is essential to the creation and refinement of a plan, or integration of it with other plans, that is, it combines forecasting of developments with the preparation of scenarios of how to react to them.

a. 6-3-5 Brainwriting
b. Planning
c. Power III
d. 180SearchAssistant

6. A _________ is a company or individual that purchases goods or services with the intention of reselling them rather than consuming or using them. This is usually done for profit (but could be resold at a loss.) One example can be found in the industry of telecommunications, where companies buy excess amounts of transmission capacity or call time from other carriers and resell it to smaller carriers.

a. Discontinuation
b. Value-based pricing
c. Reseller
d. Jobbing house

7. _________ is the practice of individuals including commercial businesses, governments and institutions, facilitating the sale of their products or services to other companies or organizations that in turn resell them, use them as components in products or services they offer _________ is also called business-to-_________ for short. (Note that while marketing to government entities shares some of the same dynamics of organizational marketing, B2G Marketing is meaningfully different.)

a. Mass marketing
b. Disruptive technology
c. Law of disruption
d. Business marketing

8. _________ is an inventory strategy implemented to improve the return on investment of a business by reducing in-process inventory and its associated carrying costs. In order to achieve JIT the process must have signals of what is going on elsewhere within the process. This means that the process is often driven by a series of signals, which can be Kanban , that tell production processes when to make the next part.

a. Clutter
b. Promotion
c. Personalization
d. Just-in-time

9. A _________, in marketing, procurement, and organizational studies, is a group of employees, family members, or members of any type of organization responsible for purchasing an item for the organization. In a business setting, major purchases typically require input from various parts of the organization, including finance, accounting, purchasing, information technology management, and senior management. Highly technical purchases, such as information systems or production equipment, also require the expertise of technical specialists.

a. Marketing myopia
b. Commercialization
c. Buying center
d. Packshot

10. _________ refers to a business or organization attempting to acquire goods or services to accomplish the goals of the enterprise. Though there are several organizations that attempt to set standards in the _________ process, processes can vary greatly between organizations. Typically the word '_________' is not used interchangeably with the word 'procurement', since procurement typically includes Expediting, Supplier Quality, and Traffic and Logistics (T'L) in addition to _________.

a. Supply network
b. Purchasing
c. Drop shipping
d. Supply chain

11. The Oxford University Press defines _________ as 'marketing on a worldwide scale reconciling or taking commercial advantage of global operational differences, similarities and opportunities in order to meet global objectives.' Oxford University Press' Glossary of Marketing Terms.

Here are three reasons for the shift from domestic to _________ as given by the authors of the textbook, _________ Management--3rd Edition by Masaaki Kotabe and Kristiaan Helsen, 2004.

One of the product categories in which global competition has been easy to track is in U.S. automotive sales.

a. Digital marketing
b. Guerrilla Marketing
c. Diversity marketing
d. Global marketing

12. _________ is an advertisement in which a particular product specifically mentions a competitor by name for the express purpose of showing why the competitor is inferior to the product naming it.

This should not be confused with parody advertisements, where a fictional product is being advertised for the purpose of poking fun at the particular advertisement, nor should it be confused with the use of a coined brand name for the purpose of comparing the product without actually naming an actual competitor. ('Wikipedia tastes better and is less filling than the Encyclopedia Galactica.')

In the 1980s, during what has been referred to as the cola wars, soft-drink manufacturer Pepsi ran a series of advertisements where people, caught on hidden camera, in a blind taste test, chose Pepsi over rival Coca-Cola.

a. Heavy-up
b. GL-70
c. Cost per conversion
d. Comparative advertising

13. In environmental modeling and especially in hydrology, a _________ model means a model that is acceptably consistent with observed natural processes, i.e. that simulates well, for example, observed river discharge. It is a key concept of the so-called Generalized Likelihood Uncertainty Estimation (GLUE) methodology to quantify how uncertain environmental predictions are.

a. 180SearchAssistant
b. Power III
c. Behavioral
d. 6-3-5 Brainwriting

14. _________ is a concept that denotes the precise probability of specific eventualities. Technically, the notion of _________ is independent from the notion of value and, as such, eventualities may have both beneficial and adverse consequences. However, in general usage the convention is to focus only on potential negative impact to some characteristic of value that may arise from a future event.

a. Power III
b. 180SearchAssistant
c. 6-3-5 Brainwriting
d. Risk

15. _________ is the set of reasons that determines one to engage in a particular behavior. The term is generally used for human _________ but, theoretically, it can be used to describe the causes for animal behavior as well

a. Motivation
b. Role playing
c. Power III
d. 180SearchAssistant

16. In business and engineering, _________ is the term used to describe the complete process of bringing a new product or service to market. There are two parallel paths involved in the _________ process: one involves the idea generation, product design, and detail engineering; the other involves market research and marketing analysis. Companies typically see _________ as the first stage in generating and commercializing new products within the overall strategic process of product life cycle management used to maintain or grow their market share.

a. Product optimization
b. Specification
c. Product development
d. New product development

17. In psychology, philosophy, and the cognitive sciences, _________ is the process of attaining awareness or understanding of sensory information. It is a task far more complex than was imagined in the 1950s and 1960s, when it was predicted that building perceiving machines would take about a decade, a goal which is still very far from fruition. The word _________ comes from the Latin words _________, percepio, meaning 'receiving, collecting, action of taking possession, apprehension with the mind or senses.'

_________ is one of the oldest fields in psychology.

a. Groupthink
b. Power III
c. Perception
d. 180SearchAssistant

18. In business and engineering, new _________ is the term used to describe the complete process of bringing a new product or service to market. There are two parallel paths involved in the Nproduct development process: one involves the idea generation, product design, and detail engineering; the other involves market research and marketing analysis. Companies typically see new _________ as the first stage in generating and commercializing new products within the overall strategic process of product life cycle management used to maintain or grow their market share.

a. Specification tree
b. New product screening
c. New product development
d. Product development

19. _________ is a broad label that refers to any individuals or households that use goods and services generated within the economy. The concept of a _________ is used in different contexts, so that the usage and significance of the term may vary.

A _________ is a person who uses any product or service.

a. Power III
b. Consumer
c. 6-3-5 Brainwriting
d. 180SearchAssistant

20. _________ can be regarded as an outcome of mental processes (cognitive process) leading to the selection of a course of action among several alternatives. Every _________ process produces a final choice. The output can be an action or an opinion of choice.

a. 180SearchAssistant
b. Decision making
c. Power III
d. 6-3-5 Brainwriting

21. _________,, is a common tool in the retail industry to create the look of a perfectly stocked store by pulling all of the products on a display or shelf to the front, as well as downstacking all the canned and stacked items. It is also done to keep the store appearing neat and organized.

The workers who face commonly have jobs doing other things in the store such as customer service, stocking shelves, daytime cleaning, bagging and carryouts, etc.

a. Facing
b. Customer Integrated System
c. Customer Experience Analytics
d. Foviance

22. _________ is a branch of philosophy which seeks to address questions about morality, such as how a moral outcome can be achieved in a specific situation (applied _________), how moral values should be determined (normative _________), what moral values people actually abide by (descriptive _________), what the fundamental semantic, ontological, and epistemic nature of _________ or morality is (meta-_________), and how moral capacity or moral agency develops and what its nature is (moral psychology.)

Socrates was one of the first Greek philosophers to encourage both scholars and the common citizen to turn their attention from the outside world to the condition of man. In this view, Knowledge having a bearing on human life was placed highest, all other knowledge being secondary.

a. Ethics
b. AMAX
c. ACNielsen
d. ADTECH

23. _________ is systematic determination of merit, worth, and significance of something or someone using criteria against a set of standards. _________ often is used to characterize and appraise subjects of interest in a wide range of human enterprises, including the arts, criminal justice, foundations and non-profit organizations, government, health care, and other human services.

Depending on the topic of interest, there are professional groups which look to the quality and rigor of the _________ process.

a. ADTECH
b. ACNielsen
c. AMAX
d. Evaluation

24. _________ refers to the methods of practicing and using another person's philosophy of business. The franchisor grants the independent operator the right to distribute its products, techniques, and trademarks for a percentage of gross monthly sales and a royalty fee. Various tangibles and intangibles such as national or international advertising, training, and other support services are commonly made available by the franchisor.

a. 180SearchAssistant
b. Power III
c. Franchise fee
d. Franchising

1. A _________ is a subgroup of people or organizations sharing one or more characteristics that cause them to have similar product and/or service needs. A true _________ meets all of the following criteria: it is distinct from other segments (different segments have different needs), it is homogeneous within the segment (exhibits common needs); it responds similarly to a market stimulus, and it can be reached by a market intervention. The term is also used when consumers with identical product and/or service needs are divided up into groups so they can be charged different amounts.

a. Commercial planning
b. Customer insight
c. Production orientation
d. Market segment

2. _________ is a marketing term, and involves evaluating the situation and trends in a particular company's market. _________ is often called the 'three c's', which refers to the three major elements that must be studied:

- Customers
- Costs
- Competition

The number of 'c's' is sometimes extended to four, five, or even six, with 'Collaboration', 'Company', and 'Competitive advantage'.

- Marketing mix
- SWOT analysis

.

a. 180SearchAssistant
b. 6-3-5 Brainwriting
c. Power III
d. Situation analysis

3. _________ is a broad label that refers to any individuals or households that use goods and services generated within the economy. The concept of a _________ is used in different contexts, so that the usage and significance of the term may vary.

A _________ is a person who uses any product or service.

a. Consumer
b. 6-3-5 Brainwriting
c. Power III
d. 180SearchAssistant

4. _________s is the social science that studies the production, distribution, and consumption of goods and services. The term _________s comes from the Ancient Greek oá¼°κονομÎ¯α from oá¼¶κος (oikos, 'house') + νÏŒμος (nomos, 'custom' or 'law'), hence 'rules of the house(hold)'. Current _________ models developed out of the broader field of political economy in the late 19th century, owing to a desire to use an empirical approach more akin to the physical sciences.

a. ACNielsen
b. Economic
c. Industrial organization
d. ADTECH

5. A _________ or digger group is a sociological group that does not constitute a politically dominant voting majority of the total population of a given society. A sociological _________ is not necessarily a numerical _________ -- it may include any group that is subnormal with respect to a dominant group in terms of social status, education, employment, wealth and political power. To avoid confusion, some writers prefer the terms 'subordinate group' and 'dominant group' rather than '_________' and 'majority', respectively.

a. Minority
b. Mociology
c. Power III
d. Reference group

6. An _________ is the manufacturing of a good or service within a category. Although _________ is a broad term for any kind of economic production, in economics and urban planning _________ is a synonym for the secondary sector, which is a type of economic activity involved in the manufacturing of raw materials into goods and products.

There are four key industrial economic sectors: the primary sector, largely raw material extraction industries such as mining and farming; the secondary sector, involving refining, construction, and manufacturing; the tertiary sector, which deals with services (such as law and medicine) and distribution of manufactured goods; and the quaternary sector, a relatively new type of knowledge _________ focusing on technological research, design and development such as computer programming, and biochemistry.

a. AMAX
b. ADTECH
c. ACNielsen
d. Industry

7. _________ is defined by the American _________ Association as the activity, set of institutions, and processes for creating, communicating, delivering, and exchanging offerings that have value for customers, clients, partners, and society at large. The term developed from the original meaning which referred literally to going to market, as in shopping, or going to a market to sell goods or services.

_________ practice tends to be seen as a creative industry, which includes advertising, distribution and selling.

a. Customer acquisition management
b. Marketing myopia
c. Product naming
d. Marketing

8. _________ is a fee paid on borrowed assets. It is the price paid for the use of borrowed money , or, money earned by deposited funds . Assets that are sometimes lent with _________ include money, shares, consumer goods through hire purchase, major assets such as aircraft, and even entire factories in finance lease arrangements.

a. AMAX
b. ACNielsen
c. ADTECH
d. Interest

9. _________ was originally coined by Austrian psychologist Alfred Adler in 1929. The current broader sense of the word dates from 1961.

In sociology, a _________ is the way a person lives.

a. Power III
b. Lifestyle
c. 6-3-5 Brainwriting
d. 180SearchAssistant

10. In the field of marketing, demographics, opinion research, and social research in general, _________ variables are any attributes relating to personality, values, attitudes, interests, or lifestyles. They are also called IAO variables . They can be contrasted with demographic variables (such as age and gender), behavioral variables (such as usage rate or loyalty), and bizographic variables (such as industry, seniority and functional area.)

a. Psychographic
b. Marketing myopia
c. Lifetime value
d. Business-to-business

11. The acronym _________, is a psychographic segmentation. It was developed in the 1970s to explain changing U.S. values and lifestyles. It has since been reworked to enhance its ability to predict consumer behavior.

According to the _________ Framework, groups of people are arranged in a rectangle and are based on two dimensions. The vertical dimension segments people based on the degree to which they are innovative and have resources such as income, education, self-confidence, intelligence, leadership skills, and energy.

a. Power III
b. 6-3-5 Brainwriting
c. VALS
d. 180SearchAssistant

12. _________ is a global marketing research firm, with worldwide headquarters in New York City. Regional headquarters for North America are located in Schaumburg, IL. As of 2008, its the part of The Nielsen Company.
a. E-Detailing
b. InfoNU
c. Alloy Entertainment
d. ACNielsen

13. _________ is a radio audience research company in the United States which collects listener data on radio audiences similar to that collected by Nielsen Media Research on television audiences. It was founded as American Research Bureau by Jim Seiler in 1949 and became bi-coastal by merging with L.A. based Coffin, Cooper and Clay in the early 1950s. ARB's initial business was the collection of television broadcast ratings exclusively.
a. Access Commerce
b. American Heart Association
c. American Cancer Society
d. Arbitron

14. Its a tool for marketing. _________ is a multivariate statistical classification technique for discovering whether the individuals of a population fall into different groups by making quantitative comparisons of multiple characteristics with the assumption that the differences within any group should be less than the differences between groups.

The information technologies employed in _________ include geographic information system and database management software.

a. Multiple discriminant analysis
b. Geodemographic segmentation
c. Principal component analysis
d. Linear discriminant analysis

15. _________ is an American firm that measures media audiences, including television, radio, theatre films (via the AMC MAP program) and newspapers. _________, headquartered in New York City and operating primarily from Chicago, is best-known for the Nielsen Ratings, a measurement of television viewership.

_________, the preeminent media research company in the world, began as a division of ACNielsen, a marketing research firm.

a. Nielsen Media Research
b. Hennes ' Mauritz
c. CoolBrands
d. Green Earth Market

16. In marketing, _________ has come to mean the process by which marketers try to create an image or identity in the minds of their target market for its product, brand, or organization. It is the 'relative competitive comparison' their product occupies in a given market as perceived by the target market.

Re-_________ involves changing the identity of a product, relative to the identity of competing products, in the collective minds of the target market.

a. Containerization
b. GE matrix
c. Moratorium
d. Positioning

17. _________ is a branch of philosophy which seeks to address questions about morality, such as how a moral outcome can be achieved in a specific situation (applied _________), how moral values should be determined (normative _________), what moral values people actually abide by (descriptive _________), what the fundamental semantic, ontological, and epistemic nature of _________ or morality is (meta-_________), and how moral capacity or moral agency develops and what its nature is (moral psychology.)

Socrates was one of the first Greek philosophers to encourage both scholars and the common citizen to turn their attention from the outside world to the condition of man. In this view, Knowledge having a bearing on human life was placed highest, all other knowledge being secondary.

a. ADTECH
b. AMAX
c. ACNielsen
d. Ethics

18. A _________ is a plan of action designed to achieve a particular goal.

_________ is different from tactics. In military terms, tactics is concerned with the conduct of an engagement while _________ is concerned with how different engagements are linked.

a. Power III
b. 180SearchAssistant
c. 6-3-5 Brainwriting
d. Strategy

1. _________ is defined by the American _________ Association as the activity, set of institutions, and processes for creating, communicating, delivering, and exchanging offerings that have value for customers, clients, partners, and society at large. The term developed from the original meaning which referred literally to going to market, as in shopping, or going to a market to sell goods or services.

_________ practice tends to be seen as a creative industry, which includes advertising, distribution and selling.

a. Customer acquisition management
b. Marketing myopia
c. Product naming
d. Marketing

2. _________ is a business discipline which is focused on the practical application of marketing techniques and the management of a firm's marketing resources and activities. Marketing managers are often responsible for influencing the level, timing, and composition of customer demand accepted definition of the term. In part, this is because the role of a marketing manager can vary significantly based on a business' size, corporate culture, and industry context.

a. Business structure
b. Performance-based advertising
c. Door-to-door
d. Marketing management

3. _________ is a term used in marketing as well as the title of an important marketing paper written by Theodore Levitt. This paper was first published in 1960 in the Harvard Business Review; a journal of which he was an editor.

Some commentators have suggested that its publication marked the beginning of the modern marketing movement.

a. Marketing performance measurement and management
b. Marketing myopia
c. Corporate image
d. Business marketing

4. _________ is an organizational lifecycle function within a company dealing with the planning or marketing of a product or products at all stages of the product lifecycle.

_________ and product marketing (outbound focused) are different yet complementary efforts with the objective of maximizing sales revenues, market share, and profit margins. The role of _________ spans many activities from strategic to tactical and varies based on the organizational structure of the company.

a. Service product management
b. Requirement prioritization
c. Product management
d. Product information management

5. A _________ is a collection of symbols, experiences and associations connected with a product, a service, a person or any other artifact or entity.

_________s have become increasingly important components of culture and the economy, now being described as 'cultural accessories and personal philosophies'.

Some people distinguish the psychological aspect of a _________ from the experiential aspect.

a. Brandable software
b. Brand equity
c. Store brand
d. Brand

6. _________ refers to the marketing effects or outcomes that accrue to a product with its brand name compared with those that would accrue if the same product did not have the brand name . And, at the root of these marketing effects is consumers' knowledge. In other words, consumers' knowledge about a brand makes manufacturers/advertisers respond differently or adopt appropriately adapt measures for the marketing of the brand .

a. Brand aversion
b. Product extension
c. Brand image
d. Brand equity

7. _________ is an advertisement in which a particular product specifically mentions a competitor by name for the express purpose of showing why the competitor is inferior to the product naming it.

This should not be confused with parody advertisements, where a fictional product is being advertised for the purpose of poking fun at the particular advertisement, nor should it be confused with the use of a coined brand name for the purpose of comparing the product without actually naming an actual competitor. ('Wikipedia tastes better and is less filling than the Encyclopedia Galactica.')

In the 1980s, during what has been referred to as the cola wars, soft-drink manufacturer Pepsi ran a series of advertisements where people, caught on hidden camera, in a blind taste test, chose Pepsi over rival Coca-Cola.

a. GL-70
b. Cost per conversion
c. Heavy-up
d. Comparative advertising

8. A _________ is a plan of action designed to achieve a particular goal.

_________ is different from tactics. In military terms, tactics is concerned with the conduct of an engagement while _________ is concerned with how different engagements are linked.

a. Power III
b. Strategy
c. 6-3-5 Brainwriting
d. 180SearchAssistant

9. A _________ is something that is acted upon or used by or by human labour or industry, for use as a building material to create some product or structure. Often the term is used to denote material that came from nature and is in an unprocessed or minimally processed state. Iron ore, logs, and crude oil, would be examples.

a. Raw material
b. Power III
c. 6-3-5 Brainwriting
d. 180SearchAssistant

10. _________ is a broad label that refers to any individuals or households that use goods and services generated within the economy. The concept of a _________ is used in different contexts, so that the usage and significance of the term may vary.

A _________ is a person who uses any product or service.

a. Power III
b. Consumer
c. 6-3-5 Brainwriting
d. 180SearchAssistant

11. _________ are final goods specifically intended for the mass market. For instance, _________ do not include investment assets, like precious antiques, even though these antiques are final goods.

Manufactured goods are goods that have been processed by way of machinery.

a. Durable good
b. Power III
c. Free good
d. Consumer goods

12. _________ is a term in economics, where demand for one good or service occurs as a result of demand for another. This may occur as the former is a part of production of the second. For example, demand for coal leads to _________ for mining, as coal must be mined for coal to be consumed.

a. 180SearchAssistant
b. Power III
c. 6-3-5 Brainwriting
d. Derived demand

13. A _________ is a market which meets a given need of a wide variety of industries, rather than a specific one.

In technology, _________s consist of customers that share a common need that exists in many or all (vertical) industries. For example, customers that need to purchase computer security services or software exist in such varied industries as finance, healthcare, government, etc.

a. Market system
b. Marketization
c. Two-sided markets
d. Horizontal market

14. _________ is a business management strategy aimed at embedding awareness of quality in all organizational processes. _________ has been widely used in manufacturing, education, call centers, government, and service industries, as well as NASA space and science programs.

When used together as a phrase, the three words in this expression have the following meanings:

- Total: Involving the entire organization, supply chain, and/or product life cycle
- Quality: With its usual definitions, with all its complexities
- Management: The system of managing with steps like Plan, Organize, Control, Lead, Staff, provisioning and organizing.

As defined by the International Organization for Standardization (ISO):

> '_________ is a management approach for an organization, centered on quality, based on the participation of all its members and aiming at long-term success through customer satisfaction, and benefits to all members of the organization and to society.' ISO 8402:1994

One major aim is to reduce variation from every process so that greater consistency of effort is obtained. (Royse, D., Thyer, B., Padgett D., ' Logan T., 2006)

In Japan, _________ comprises four process steps, namely:

1. Kaizen - Focuses on 'Continuous Process Improvement', to make processes visible, repeatable and measurable.
2. Atarimae Hinshitsu - The idea that 'things will work as they are supposed to' .
3. Kansei - Examining the way the user applies the product leads to improvement in the product itself.
4. Miryokuteki Hinshitsu - The idea that 'things should have an aesthetic quality' (for example, a pen will write in a way that is pleasing to the writer.)

_________ requires that the company maintain this quality standard in all aspects of its business. This requires ensuring that things are done right the first time and that defects and waste are eliminated from operations.

a. 6-3-5 Brainwriting
b. Total quality management
c. Power III
d. 180SearchAssistant

15. A _________ is a group of similar businesses and customers which engage in trade based on specific and specialized needs. Often, participants in a _________ are very limited to a subset of a larger industry (a niche market.) An example of this sort of market is the market for point-of-sale terminals, which are often designed specifically for similar customers and are not available for purchase to the general public.

a. Production orientation
b. Marketing myopia
c. Buy one, get one free
d. Vertical market

16. In economics, _________ is the desire to own something and the ability to pay for it. The term _________ signifies the ability or the willingness to buy a particular commodity at a given point of time .

.

a. Discretionary spending
b. Market dominance
c. Market system
d. Demand

17. _________ refers to a business or organization attempting to acquire goods or services to accomplish the goals of the enterprise. Though there are several organizations that attempt to set standards in the _________ process, processes can vary greatly between organizations. Typically the word '_________' is not used interchangeably with the word 'procurement', since procurement typically includes Expediting, Supplier Quality, and Traffic and Logistics (T'L) in addition to _________.

a. Supply network
b. Supply chain
c. Drop shipping
d. Purchasing

18. A personal and cultural _________ is a relative ethic _________, an assumption upon which implementation can be extrapolated. A _________ system is a set of consistent _________s and measures that is soo not true. A principle _________ is a foundation upon which other _________s and measures of integrity are based.

a. Supreme Court of the United States
b. Perceptual maps
c. Value
d. Package-on-Package

19. _________ is a rivalry between individuals, groups, nations for territory, a niche, or allocation of resources. It arises whenever two or more parties strive for a goal which cannot be shared. _________ occurs naturally between living organisms which co-exist in the same environment.

a. Price fixing
b. Price competition
c. Non-price competition
d. Competition

20. _________ is one of the four elements of marketing mix. An organization or set of organizations (go-betweens) involved in the process of making a product or service available for use or consumption by a consumer or business user.

The other three parts of the marketing mix are product, pricing, and promotion.

a. Japan Advertising Photographers' Association
b. Better Living Through Chemistry
c. Comparison-Shopping agent
d. Distribution

21. Procter is a surname, and may also refer to:

- Bryan Waller Procter (pseud. Barry Cornwall), English poet
- Goodwin Procter, American law firm
- _________, consumer products multinational

.

a. Convergent
b. Flyer
c. Black PRies
d. Procter ' Gamble

22. There are many important decisions about product and service development and marketing. In the process of product development and marketing we should focus on strategic decisions about product attributes, product branding, product packaging, product labeling and product support services. But product strategy also calls for building a _________.

a. Macromarketing
b. Technology acceptance model
c. Pinstorm
d. Product line

23. In economics, business, retail, and accounting, a _________ is the value of money that has been used up to produce something, and hence is not available for use anymore. In economics, a _________ is an alternative that is given up as a result of a decision. In business, the _________ may be one of acquisition, in which case the amount of money expended to acquire it is counted as _________.

a. Fixed costs
b. Transaction cost
c. Variable cost
d. Cost

24. In psychology, philosophy, and the cognitive sciences, _________ is the process of attaining awareness or understanding of sensory information. It is a task far more complex than was imagined in the 1950s and 1960s, when it was predicted that building perceiving machines would take about a decade, a goal which is still very far from fruition. The word _________ comes from the Latin words _________, percepio, meaning 'receiving, collecting, action of taking possession, apprehension with the mind or senses.'

_________ is one of the oldest fields in psychology.

a. Groupthink
b. Power III
c. 180SearchAssistant
d. Perception

25. _________ is anything that is intended to save time, energy or frustration. A _________ store at a petrol station, for example, sells items that have nothing to do with gasoline/petrol, but it saves the consumer from having to go to a grocery store. '_________' is a very relative term and its meaning tends to change over time.

a. Convenience
b. Demographic profile
c. MaxDiff
d. Marketing buzz

26. _________ is the examining of goods or services from retailers with the intent to purchase at that time. _________ is an activity of selection and/or purchase. In some contexts it is considered a leisure activity as well as an economic one.

a. Khodebshchik
b. Shopping
c. Discount store
d. Hawkers

27. A _________ or trade mark, identified by the symbols â„¢ (not yet registered) and Â® (registered) business organization or other legal entity to identify that the products and/or services to consumers with which the _________ appears originate from a unique source of origin, and to distinguish its products or services from those of other entities. A _________ is a type of intellectual property, and typically a name, word, phrase, logo, symbol, design, image, or a combination of these elements. There is also a range of non-conventional _________s comprising marks which do not fall into these standard categories.

a. Power III
b. Trademark
c. Risk management
d. 180SearchAssistant

28. _________ or brand stretching is a marketing strategy in which a firm marketing a product with a well-developed image uses the same brand name in a different product category. Organizations use this strategy to increase and leverage brand equity (definition: the net worth and long-term sustainability just from the renowned name.) An example of a _________ is Jello-gelatin creating Jello pudding pops.

a. Brand orientation
b. Brand awareness
c. Web 2.0
d. Brand extension

29. A product _________ is the use of an established product's brand name for a new item in the same product category._________s occur when a company introduces additional items in the same product category under the same brand name such as new flavors, forms, colors, added ingredients, package sizes.Examples includei) Zen LXI, Zen VXIii) Surf, Surf Excel, Surf Excel Blueiii) Splendour, Splendour Plusiv) Coke, Diet Coke, Vanilla Cokev) Clinic All Clear, Clinic Plus

- brand
- brand management
- marketing
- product management
- Product lining

.

a. Line extension
b. Brand Development Index
c. Perishability
d. Targeted advertising

30. _________ is the marketing strategy of giving each product in a product portfolio its own unique brand name. This is contrasted with family branding in which the products in a product line are given the same brand name. The advantage of _________ is that each product has a self image and identity that's unique.

a. Intangibility
b. Individual branding
c. Online focus group
d. Engagement

31. _________ is a marketing strategy that involves selling several related products under one brand name. It is contrasted with individual branding in which each product in a portfolio is given a unique identity and brand name.

There are often economies of scope associated with _________ since several products can efficiently be promoted with a single advertisement or campaign.

a. Family branding
b. Power III
c. 6-3-5 Brainwriting
d. 180SearchAssistant

32. _________, in marketing, consists of a consumer's commitment to repurchase the brand and can be demonstrated by repeated buying of a product or service or other positive behaviors such as word of mouth advocacy. True _________ implies that the consumer is willing, at least on occasion, to put aside their own desires in the interest of the brand. _________ has been proclaimed by some to be the ultimate goal of marketing.

a. Brand awareness
b. Brand implementation
c. Trade Symbols
d. Brand loyalty

33. _________ is a measure of the strength of a brand, product, service relative to competitive offerings. There is often a geographic element to the competitive landscape. In defining _________, you must see to what extent a product, brand, or firm controls a product category in a given geographic area.

a. Productivity
b. Market dominance
c. Discretionary spending
d. Market system

34. In marketing, _________ has come to mean the process by which marketers try to create an image or identity in the minds of their target market for its product, brand, or organization. It is the 'relative competitive comparison' their product occupies in a given market as perceived by the target market.

Re-_________ involves changing the identity of a product, relative to the identity of competing products, in the collective minds of the target market.

a. Positioning
b. Moratorium
c. GE matrix
d. Containerization

35. _________ is a technique used in propaganda and advertising. Also known as association, this is a technique of projecting positive or negative qualities (praise or blame) of a person, entity, object, or value (an individual, group, organization, nation, patriotism, etc.) to another in order to make the second more acceptable or to discredit it.

a. Supplier
b. Sexism,
c. Micro ads
d. Transfer

36. _________, in strategic management and marketing, is the percentage or proportion of the total available market or market segment that is being serviced by a company. It can be expressed as a company's sales revenue (from that market) divided by the total sales revenue available in that market. It can also be expressed as a company's unit sales volume (in a market) divided by the total volume of units sold in that market.

a. Customer relationship management
b. Cyberdoc
c. Demand generation
d. Market share

37. The _________ is generally accepted as the use and specification of the four p's describing the strategic position of a product in the marketplace. One version of the origins of the _________ starts in 1948 when James Culliton said that a marketing decision should be a result of something similar to a recipe. This version continued in 1953 when Neil Borden, in his American Marketing Association presidential address, took the recipe idea one step further and coined the term 'Marketing-Mix'.

a. Power III
b. 180SearchAssistant
c. Marketing mix
d. 6-3-5 Brainwriting

38. _________ Management is the succession of strategies used by management as a product goes through its _________. The conditions in which a product is sold changes over time and must be managed as it moves through its succession of stages.

The _________ goes through many phases, involves many professional disciplines, and requires many skills, tools and processes.

a. Customer satisfaction
b. Supplier diversity
c. Chain stores
d. Product life cycle

39. A _________ is a process that can allow an organization to concentrate its limited resources on the greatest opportunities to increase sales and achieve a sustainable competitive advantage. A _________ should be centered around the key concept that customer satisfaction is the main goal.

A _________ is most effective when it is an integral component of corporate strategy, defining how the organization will successfully engage customers, prospects, and competitors in the market arena.

a. Societal marketing
b. Psychographic
c. Cyberdoc
d. Marketing strategy

40. _________ is one of the four Ps of the marketing mix. The other three aspects are product, promotion, and place. It is also a key variable in microeconomic price allocation theory.

a. Relationship based pricing
b. Competitor indexing
c. Price
d. Pricing

41. A craze is a product, idea, cultural movement, or model that gains popularity among a small section of the populace then quickly migrates to the mainstream. Crazes are characterized by their lightning fast adoption and swift departure from public awareness. Crazes and _________s are also characterized by their unusually high interest and sales figures relative to the time they are active in the marketplace, as compared with other similar products, ideas, cultural movements or models.

a. 180SearchAssistant
b. Fad
c. 6-3-5 Brainwriting
d. Power III

42. _________ is the process by which a new idea or new product is accepted by the market. The rate of _________ is the speed that the new idea spreads from one consumer to the next. Adoption is similar to _________ except that it deals with the psychological processes an individual goes through, rather than an aggregate market process.

a. Market development
b. Perceptual maps
c. Diffusion
d. Kano model

43. The general definition of an _________ is an evaluation of a person, organization, system, process, project or product. _________s are performed to ascertain the validity and reliability of information; also to provide an assessment of a system's internal control. The goal of an _________ is to express an opinion on the person/organization/system (etc) in question, under evaluation based on work done on a test basis.

a. ACNielsen
b. Audit
c. ADTECH
d. AMAX

44. _________ is the process of comparing the cost, cycle time, productivity, or quality of a specific process or method to another that is widely considered to be an industry standard or best practice. The result is often a business case for making changes in order to make improvements. The term _________ was first used by cobblers to measure ones feet for shoes.

a. Strategic group
b. Switching cost
c. Business strategy
d. Benchmarking

45. _________ is a retailing concept in which the total range of products sold by a retailer is broken down into discrete groups of similar or related products; these groups are known as product categories. Examples of grocery categories may be: tinned fish, washing detergent, toothpastes, etc.Each category is then run like a 'mini business' (Business Unit) in its own right, with its own set of turnover and/or profitability targets and strategies. An important facet of _________ is the shift in relationship between retailer and supplier : instead of the traditional adversarial relationship, the relationship moves to one of collaboration, exchange of information and data and joint business building.The focus of all negotiations is centered around the effects of the turnover of the total category, not just the sales on the individual products therein.

a. Category management
b. Societal marketing
c. Market segment
d. Brochure

46. A _________ is a group of employees from various functional areas of the organization - research, engineering, marketing, finance. human resources, and operations, for example - who are all focused on a specific objective and are responsible to work as a team to improve coordination and innovation across divisions and resolve mutual problems.

a. Job analysis
b. Cross-functional team
c. 180SearchAssistant
d. Power III

47. Levi Strauss, born Löb Strauss (February 26, 1829 - September 26, 1902) was a German-Jewish immigrant to the United States who founded the first company to manufacture blue jeans. His firm, _________, began in 1853 in San Francisco, California.

Levi Strauss was born in Bavaria, Germany, to Hirsch Strauss and his wife Rebecca (Haas) Strauss.

a. AStore
b. Albert Einstein
c. African Americans
d. Levi Strauss ' Company

48. _________ is a global document management company which manufactures and sells a range of color and black-and-white printers, multifunction systems, photo copiers, digital production printing presses, and related consulting services and supplies. Xerox is headquartered in Norwalk, Connecticut , though its largest population of employees is based in and around Rochester, New York, the area in which the company was founded. The Xerox 914 was the first one-piece plain paper photocopier, and sold in the thousands.

Xerox was founded in 1906 in Rochester, New York as 'The Haloid Company', which originally manufactured photographic paper and equipment.

a. Partnership for a Drug-Free America
b. Japan Advertising Photographers' Association
c. Green Earth Market
d. Xerox Corporation

49. In business and engineering, _________ is the term used to describe the complete process of bringing a new product or service to market. There are two parallel paths involved in the _________ process: one involves the idea generation, product design, and detail engineering; the other involves market research and marketing analysis. Companies typically see _________ as the first stage in generating and commercializing new products within the overall strategic process of product life cycle management used to maintain or grow their market share.

a. Product optimization
b. Product development
c. New product development
d. Specification

50. In business and engineering, new _________ is the term used to describe the complete process of bringing a new product or service to market. There are two parallel paths involved in the Nproduct development process: one involves the idea generation, product design, and detail engineering; the other involves market research and marketing analysis. Companies typically see new _________ as the first stage in generating and commercializing new products within the overall strategic process of product life cycle management used to maintain or grow their market share.

a. New product development
b. New product screening
c. Product development
d. Specification tree

1. A _________ is a collection of symbols, experiences and associations connected with a product, a service, a person or any other artifact or entity.

_________s have become increasingly important components of culture and the economy, now being described as 'cultural accessories and personal philosophies'.

Some people distinguish the psychological aspect of a _________ from the experiential aspect.

a. Store brand
b. Brand
c. Brand equity
d. Brandable software

2. Competitiveness is a comparative concept of the ability and performance of a firm, sub-sector or country to sell and supply goods and/or services in a given market. Although widely used in economics and business management, the usefulness of the concept, particularly in the context of national competitiveness, is vigorously disputed by economists, such as Paul Krugman .

The term may also be applied to markets, where it is used to refer to the extent to which the market structure may be regarded as perfectly _________.

a. Geographical pricing
b. Customs union
c. Competitive
d. Free trade zone

3. In economics, business, retail, and accounting, a _________ is the value of money that has been used up to produce something, and hence is not available for use anymore. In economics, a _________ is an alternative that is given up as a result of a decision. In business, the _________ may be one of acquisition, in which case the amount of money expended to acquire it is counted as _________.

a. Transaction cost
b. Cost
c. Variable cost
d. Fixed costs

4. _________ or economic opportunity loss is the value of the next best alternative forgone as the result of making a decision. _________ analysis is an important part of a company's decision-making processes but is not treated as an actual cost in any financial statement. The next best thing that a person can engage in is referred to as the _________ of doing the best thing and ignoring the next best thing to be done.

a. Opportunity cost
b. AMAX
c. ACNielsen
d. ADTECH

5. Procter is a surname, and may also refer to:

- Bryan Waller Procter (pseud. Barry Cornwall), English poet
- Goodwin Procter, American law firm
- _________, consumer products multinational

.

a. Procter ' Gamble
b. Flyer
c. Black PRies
d. Convergent

6. In economics, _________ is the desire to own something and the ability to pay for it. The term _________ signifies the ability or the willingness to buy a particular commodity at a given point of time .

.

a. Market dominance
b. Market system
c. Discretionary spending
d. Demand

7. _________ is one of the four Ps of the marketing mix. The other three aspects are product, promotion, and place. It is also a key variable in microeconomic price allocation theory.

a. Competitor indexing
b. Price
c. Relationship based pricing
d. Pricing

8. A _________ is a plan of action designed to achieve a particular goal.

_________ is different from tactics. In military terms, tactics is concerned with the conduct of an engagement while _________ is concerned with how different engagements are linked.

a. 6-3-5 Brainwriting
b. Strategy
c. Power III
d. 180SearchAssistant

9. A product _________ is the use of an established product's brand name for a new item in the same product category._________s occur when a company introduces additional items in the same product category under the same brand name such as new flavors, forms, colors, added ingredients, package sizes.Examples includei) Zen LXI, Zen VXIii) Surf, Surf Excel, Surf Excel Blueiii) Splendour, Splendour Plusiv) Coke, Diet Coke, Vanilla Cokev) Clinic All Clear, Clinic Plus

- brand
- brand management
- marketing
- product management
- Product lining

.

a. Perishability
b. Targeted advertising
c. Brand Development Index
d. Line extension

10. A _________ strategy targets non-buying customers in currently targeted segments. It also targets new customers in new segments. (Winer)

A marketing manager has to think about the following questions before implementing a _________ strategy: Is it profitable? Will it require the introduction of new or modified products? Is the customer and channel well enough researched and understood?

The marketing manager uses these four groups to give more focus to the market segment decision: existing customers, competitor customers, non-buying in current segments, new segments.

a. Market development
b. Commercial planning
c. Kano model
d. Perceptual mapping

11. _________ is one of the four growth strategies of the Product-Market Growth Matrix defined by Ansoff. _________ occurs when a company enters/penetrates a market with current products. The best way to achieve this is by gaining competitors' customers (part of their market share.)

a. Horizontal market
b. Pasar pagi
c. Marketization
d. Market penetration

12. There are many important decisions about product and service development and marketing. In the process of product development and marketing we should focus on strategic decisions about product attributes, product branding, product packaging, product labeling and product support services. But product strategy also calls for building a _________.

a. Pinstorm
b. Macromarketing
c. Technology acceptance model
d. Product line

13. _________s is the social science that studies the production, distribution, and consumption of goods and services. The term _________s comes from the Ancient Greek oá¼°κονομÎ¯α from oá¼¶κος (oikos, 'house') + νÏŒμος (nomos, 'custom' or 'law'), hence 'rules of the house(hold)'. Current _________ models developed out of the broader field of political economy in the late 19th century, owing to a desire to use an empirical approach more akin to the physical sciences.

a. ADTECH
b. ACNielsen
c. Industrial organization
d. Economic

14. _________ is a branch of philosophy which seeks to address questions about morality, such as how a moral outcome can be achieved in a specific situation (applied _________), how moral values should be determined (normative _________), what moral values people actually abide by (descriptive _________), what the fundamental semantic, ontological, and epistemic nature of _________ or morality is (meta-_________), and how moral capacity or moral agency develops and what its nature is (moral psychology.)

Socrates was one of the first Greek philosophers to encourage both scholars and the common citizen to turn their attention from the outside world to the condition of man. In this view, Knowledge having a bearing on human life was placed highest, all other knowledge being secondary.

a. Ethics
b. AMAX
c. ADTECH
d. ACNielsen

15. _________ is defined by the American _________ Association as the activity, set of institutions, and processes for creating, communicating, delivering, and exchanging offerings that have value for customers, clients, partners, and society at large. The term developed from the original meaning which referred literally to going to market, as in shopping, or going to a market to sell goods or services.

_________ practice tends to be seen as a creative industry, which includes advertising, distribution and selling.

a. Marketing
b. Marketing myopia
c. Customer acquisition management
d. Product naming

16. A _________ is a process that can allow an organization to concentrate its limited resources on the greatest opportunities to increase sales and achieve a sustainable competitive advantage. A _________ should be centered around the key concept that customer satisfaction is the main goal.

A _________ is most effective when it is an integral component of corporate strategy, defining how the organization will successfully engage customers, prospects, and competitors in the market arena.

a. Marketing strategy
b. Cyberdoc
c. Psychographic
d. Societal marketing

17. In economic models, the _________ time frame assumes no fixed factors of production. Firms can enter or leave the marketplace, and the cost (and availability) of land, labor, raw materials, and capital goods can be assumed to vary. In contrast, in the short-run time frame, certain factors are assumed to be fixed, because there is not sufficient time for them to change.

a. 180SearchAssistant
b. Power III
c. Long-run
d. 6-3-5 Brainwriting

18. The business terms _________ and pull originated in the logistic and supply chain management, but are also widely used in marketing.

A _________-pull-system in business describes the move of a product or information between two subjects. On markets the consumers usually 'pulls' the goods or information they demand for their needs, while the offerers or suppliers '_________es' them toward the consumers.

a. Gold Key Matching Service
b. Completely randomized designs
c. Manufacturers' representatives
d. Push

19. _________ is the risk that the value of an investment will decrease due to moves in market factors. The four standard _________ factors are:

- Equity risk, the risk that stock prices will change.
- Interest rate risk, the risk that interest rates will change.
- Currency risk, the risk that foreign exchange rates will change.
- Commodity risk, the risk that commodity prices (e.g. grains, metals) will change.

As with other forms of risk, _________ may be measured in a number of ways. Traditionally, this is done using a Value at Risk methodology. Value at risk is well established as a risk management technique, but it contains a number of limiting assumptions that constrain its accuracy.

a. 6-3-5 Brainwriting
b. 180SearchAssistant
c. Power III
d. Market risk

20. _________ is part of project management, which relates to the use of schedules such as Gantt charts to plan and subsequently report progress within the project environment.

Initially, the project scope is defined and the appropriate methods for completing the project are determined. Following this step, the durations for the various tasks necessary to complete the work are listed and grouped into a work breakdown structure.

a. Project planning
b. Power III
c. 180SearchAssistant
d. Product breakdown structure

21. _________ is a concept that denotes the precise probability of specific eventualities. Technically, the notion of _________ is independent from the notion of value and, as such, eventualities may have both beneficial and adverse consequences. However, in general usage the convention is to focus only on potential negative impact to some characteristic of value that may arise from a future event.

a. 6-3-5 Brainwriting
b. Risk
c. Power III
d. 180SearchAssistant

22. _________ is systematic determination of merit, worth, and significance of something or someone using criteria against a set of standards. _________ often is used to characterize and appraise subjects of interest in a wide range of human enterprises, including the arts, criminal justice, foundations and non-profit organizations, government, health care, and other human services.

Depending on the topic of interest, there are professional groups which look to the quality and rigor of the _________ process.

a. AMAX
b. Evaluation
c. ACNielsen
d. ADTECH

23. In business and engineering, _________ is the term used to describe the complete process of bringing a new product or service to market. There are two parallel paths involved in the _________ process: one involves the idea generation, product design, and detail engineering; the other involves market research and marketing analysis. Companies typically see _________ as the first stage in generating and commercializing new products within the overall strategic process of product life cycle management used to maintain or grow their market share.

a. Product optimization
b. Product development
c. Specification
d. New product development

24. _________ in organizations and public policy is both the organizational process of creating and maintaining a plan; and the psychological process of thinking about the activities required to create a desired goal on some scale. As such, it is a fundamental property of intelligent behavior. This thought process is essential to the creation and refinement of a plan, or integration of it with other plans, that is, it combines forecasting of developments with the preparation of scenarios of how to react to them.

a. 180SearchAssistant
b. 6-3-5 Brainwriting
c. Power III
d. Planning

25. In business and engineering, new _________ is the term used to describe the complete process of bringing a new product or service to market. There are two parallel paths involved in the Nproduct development process: one involves the idea generation, product design, and detail engineering; the other involves market research and marketing analysis. Companies typically see new _________ as the first stage in generating and commercializing new products within the overall strategic process of product life cycle management used to maintain or grow their market share.

a. New product screening
b. Specification tree
c. New product development
d. Product development

26. _________ is a broad label that refers to any individuals or households that use goods and services generated within the economy. The concept of a _________ is used in different contexts, so that the usage and significance of the term may vary.

A _________ is a person who uses any product or service.

a. Power III
b. 6-3-5 Brainwriting
c. Consumer
d. 180SearchAssistant

27. A _________ is a group of employees from various functional areas of the organization - research, engineering, marketing, finance. human resources, and operations, for example - who are all focused on a specific objective and are responsible to work as a team to improve coordination and innovation across divisions and resolve mutual problems.

a. 180SearchAssistant
b. Power III
c. Job analysis
d. Cross-functional team

28. A _________, in the field of business and marketing, is a geographic region or demographic group used to gauge the viability of a product or service in the mass market prior to a wide scale roll-out. The criteria used to judge the acceptability of a _________ region or group include:

1. a population that is demographically similar to the proposed target market; and
2. relative isolation from densely populated media markets so that advertising to the test audience can be efficient and economical.

The _________ ideally aims to duplicate 'everything' - promotion and distribution as well as `product' - on a smaller scale. The technique replicates, typically in one area, what is planned to occur in a national launch; and the results are very carefully monitored, so that they can be extrapolated to projected national results. The `area' may be any one of the following:

- Television area
- Test town
- Residential neighborhood
- Test site

A number of decisions have to be taken about any _________:

- Which _________?
- What is to be tested?
- How long a test?
- What are the success criteria?

The simple go or no-go decision, together with the related reduction of risk, is normally the main justification for the expense of _________s. At the same time, however, such _________s can be used to test specific elements of a new product's marketing mix; possibly the version of the product itself, the promotional message and media spend, the distribution channels and the price.

a. Preadolescence b. 180SearchAssistant
c. Test market d. Power III

29. _________ is a form of communication that typically attempts to persuade potential customers to purchase or to consume more of a particular brand of product or service. 'While now central to the contemporary global economy and the reproduction of global production networks, it is only quite recently that _________ has been more than a marginal influence on patterns of sales and production. The formation of modern _________ was intimately bound up with the emergence of new forms of monopoly capitalism around the end of the 19th and beginning of the 20th century as one element in corporate strategies to create, organize and where possible control markets, especially for mass produced consumer goods.
a. ADTECH b. ACNielsen
c. Advertising d. AMAX

30. _________ generally refers to a list of all planned expenses and revenues. It is a plan for saving and spending. A _________ is an important concept in microeconomics, which uses a _________ line to illustrate the trade-offs between two or more goods.
a. 180SearchAssistant b. Power III
c. 6-3-5 Brainwriting d. Budget

31. In economics, an externality or spillover of an economic transaction is an impact on a party that is not directly involved in the transaction. In such a case, prices do not reflect the full costs or benefits in production or consumption of a product or service. A positive impact is called an _________ benefit, while a negative impact is called an _________ cost.
a. ADTECH b. AMAX
c. ACNielsen d. External

32. _________ is the process or cycle of introducing a new product into the market. The actual launch of a new product is the final stage of new product development, and the one where the most money will have to be spent for advertising, sales promotion, and other marketing efforts. In the case of a new consumer packaged good, costs will be at least $ 10 million, but can reach up to $ 200 million.
a. Confusion marketing b. Sweepstakes
c. Customer Interaction Tracker d. Commercialization

33. An _________ is a person who creates or discovers a new method, form, device or other useful means. The word _________ comes form the latin verb invenire, invent-, to find. The system of patents was established to encourage _________s by granting limited-term, limited monopoly on inventions determined to be sufficiently novel, non-obvious, and useful.

a. AMAX
b. ACNielsen
c. Inventor
d. ADTECH

34. In commerce, _________ is the length of time it takes from a product being conceived until its being available for sale. _________ is important in industries where products are outmoded quickly. A common assumption is that _________ matters most for first-of-a-kind products, but actually the leader often has the luxury of time, while the clock is clearly running for the followers.

a. Time to market
b. Product support
c. Customer centricity
d. Product life cycle management

35. _________ is the ongoing process of identifying and articulating market requirements that define a product's feature set.

a. Brand parity
b. Targeted advertising
c. Market intelligence
d. Product planning

36. _________ is, in very basic words, a position a firm occupies against its competitors.

According to Michael Porter, the three methods for creating a sustainable _________ are through:

1. Cost leadership - Cost advantage occurs when a firm delivers the same services as its competitors but at a lower cost;

2.

a. 6-3-5 Brainwriting
b. Power III
c. 180SearchAssistant
d. Competitive advantage

37. _________ can be defined as the idea generation, concept development, testing and manufacturing or implementation of a physical object or service. _________ers conceptualize and evaluate ideas, making them tangible through products in a more systematic approach. The role of a _________er encompasses many characteristics of the marketing manager, product manager, industrial designer and design engineer.

a. Albert Einstein
b. African Americans
c. AStore
d. Product design

38. _________ is an advertisement in which a particular product specifically mentions a competitor by name for the express purpose of showing why the competitor is inferior to the product naming it.

This should not be confused with parody advertisements, where a fictional product is being advertised for the purpose of poking fun at the particular advertisement, nor should it be confused with the use of a coined brand name for the purpose of comparing the product without actually naming an actual competitor. ('Wikipedia tastes better and is less filling than the Encyclopedia Galactica.')

In the 1980s, during what has been referred to as the cola wars, soft-drink manufacturer Pepsi ran a series of advertisements where people, caught on hidden camera, in a blind taste test, chose Pepsi over rival Coca-Cola.

a. Heavy-up
b. Cost per conversion
c. GL-70
d. Comparative advertising

39. In psychology, philosophy, and the cognitive sciences, _________ is the process of attaining awareness or understanding of sensory information. It is a task far more complex than was imagined in the 1950s and 1960s, when it was predicted that building perceiving machines would take about a decade, a goal which is still very far from fruition. The word _________ comes from the Latin words _________, percepio, meaning 'receiving, collecting, action of taking possession, apprehension with the mind or senses.'

_________ is one of the oldest fields in psychology.

a. 180SearchAssistant
b. Groupthink
c. Power III
d. Perception

40. A personal and cultural _________ is a relative ethic _________, an assumption upon which implementation can be extrapolated. A _________ system is a set of consistent _________s and measures that is soo not true. A principle _________ is a foundation upon which other _________s and measures of integrity are based.

a. Supreme Court of the United States
b. Package-on-Package
c. Perceptual maps
d. Value

1. _________ , according to The American Marketing Association, is 'a planning process designed to assure that all brand contacts received by a customer or prospect for a product, service, or organization are relevant to that person and consistent over time.' (Marketing Power Dictionary)

_________ is a term used to describe a holistic approach to marketing. It aims to ensure consistency of message and the complementary use of media. The concept includes online and offline marketing channels.

a. ADTECH
b. Integrated marketing communications
c. AMAX
d. ACNielsen

2. _________ is a form of communication that typically attempts to persuade potential customers to purchase or to consume more of a particular brand of product or service. 'While now central to the contemporary global economy and the reproduction of global production networks, it is only quite recently that _________ has been more than a marginal influence on patterns of sales and production. The formation of modern _________ was intimately bound up with the emergence of new forms of monopoly capitalism around the end of the 19th and beginning of the 20th century as one element in corporate strategies to create, organize and where possible control markets, especially for mass produced consumer goods.

a. ACNielsen
b. Advertising
c. AMAX
d. ADTECH

3. _________ is defined by the American _________ Association as the activity, set of institutions, and processes for creating, communicating, delivering, and exchanging offerings that have value for customers, clients, partners, and society at large. The term developed from the original meaning which referred literally to going to market, as in shopping, or going to a market to sell goods or services.

_________ practice tends to be seen as a creative industry, which includes advertising, distribution and selling.

a. Marketing myopia
b. Customer acquisition management
c. Product naming
d. Marketing

4. _________ refers to messages and related media used to communicate with a market. Those who practice advertising, branding, direct marketing, graphic design, marketing, packaging, promotion, publicity, sponsorship, public relations, sales, sales promotion and online marketing are termed marketing communicators, _________ managers, or more briefly as marcom managers.

a. Sales promotion
b. Merchandise
c. Marketing communication
d. Merchandising

5. _________ is a broad label that refers to any individuals or households that use goods and services generated within the economy. The concept of a _________ is used in different contexts, so that the usage and significance of the term may vary.

A _________ is a person who uses any product or service.

a. 6-3-5 Brainwriting
b. Power III
c. Consumer
d. 180SearchAssistant

6. _________ involves disseminating information about a product, product line, brand, or company. It is one of the four key aspects of the marketing mix. (The other three elements are product marketing, pricing, and distribution). P>_________ is generally sub-divided into two parts:

- Above the line _________: Promotion in the media (e.g. TV, radio, newspapers, Internet and Mobile Phones) in which the advertiser pays an advertising agency to place the ad
- Below the line _________: All other _________. Much of this is intended to be subtle enough for the consumer to be unaware that _________ is taking place. E.g. sponsorship, product placement, endorsements, sales _________, merchandising, direct mail, personal selling, public relations, trade shows

a. Cashmere Agency
b. Davie Brown Index
c. Bottling lines
d. Promotion

7. _________ is a sub-discipline and type of marketing. There are two main definitional characteristics which distinguish it from other types of marketing. The first is that it attempts to send its messages directly to consumers, without the use of intervening media.

a. Database marketing
b. Power III
c. Direct Marketing Associations
d. Direct marketing

8. _________ is the practice of managing the flow of information between an organization and its publics. _________ - often referred to as _________ - gains an organization or individual exposure to their audiences using topics of public interest and news items that do not require direct payment. Because _________ places exposure in credible third-party outlets, it offers a third-party legitimacy that advertising does not have.

a. Symbolic analysis
b. Graphic communication
c. Power III
d. Public relations

9. A _________ is a systematic approach to selling a product or service. A growing body of published literature approaches the _________ from the point of view of an engineering discipline

Reasons for having a well thought-out _________ include seller and buyer risk management, standardized customer interaction in sales, and scalable revenue generation.

a. Lead generation
b. Request for proposal
c. Sales management
d. Sales process

10. _________ is one of the four aspects of promotional mix. (The other three parts of the promotional mix are advertising, personal selling, and publicity/public relations.) Media and non-media marketing communication are employed for a pre-determined, limited time to increase consumer demand, stimulate market demand or improve product availability.

a. Marketing communication
b. New Media Strategies
c. Sales promotion
d. Merchandise

11. _________ is the study of when, why, how, where and what people do or do not buy products. It blends elements from psychology, sociology,social psychology, anthropology and economics. It attempts to understand the buyer decision making process, both individually and in groups. It studies characteristics of individual consumers such as demographics and behavioural variables in an attempt to understand people's wants. It also tries to assess influences on the consumer from groups such as family, friends, reference groups, and society in general.

a. Communal marketing
b. Consumer confidence
c. Multidimensional scaling
d. Consumer behavior

12. A personal and cultural _________ is a relative ethic _________, an assumption upon which implementation can be extrapolated. A _________ system is a set of consistent _________s and measures that is soo not true. A principle _________ is a foundation upon which other _________s and measures of integrity are based.

a. Supreme Court of the United States
b. Perceptual maps
c. Value
d. Package-on-Package

13. _________ is a radio audience research company in the United States which collects listener data on radio audiences similar to that collected by Nielsen Media Research on television audiences. It was founded as American Research Bureau by Jim Seiler in 1949 and became bi-coastal by merging with L.A. based Coffin, Cooper and Clay in the early 1950s. ARB's initial business was the collection of television broadcast ratings exclusively.

a. American Cancer Society
b. American Heart Association
c. Arbitron
d. Access Commerce

14. _________ generally refers to a list of all planned expenses and revenues. It is a plan for saving and spending. A _________ is an important concept in microeconomics, which uses a _________ line to illustrate the trade-offs between two or more goods.

a. Power III
b. Budget
c. 180SearchAssistant
d. 6-3-5 Brainwriting

15. A _________ is a collection of symbols, experiences and associations connected with a product, a service, a person or any other artifact or entity.

_________s have become increasingly important components of culture and the economy, now being described as 'cultural accessories and personal philosophies'.

Some people distinguish the psychological aspect of a _________ from the experiential aspect.

a. Brand equity
b. Brand
c. Store brand
d. Brandable software

16. _________ refers to the marketing effects or outcomes that accrue to a product with its brand name compared with those that would accrue if the same product did not have the brand name . And, at the root of these marketing effects is consumers' knowledge. In other words, consumers' knowledge about a brand makes manufacturers/advertisers respond differently or adopt appropriately adapt measures for the marketing of the brand .

a. Brand aversion
b. Brand image
c. Product extension
d. Brand equity

17. _________, in strategic management and marketing, is the percentage or proportion of the total available market or market segment that is being serviced by a company. It can be expressed as a company's sales revenue (from that market) divided by the total sales revenue available in that market. It can also be expressed as a company's unit sales volume (in a market) divided by the total volume of units sold in that market.

a. Cyberdoc
b. Customer relationship management
c. Demand generation
d. Market share

18. Procter is a surname, and may also refer to:

- Bryan Waller Procter (pseud. Barry Cornwall), English poet
- Goodwin Procter, American law firm
- _________, consumer products multinational

.

a. Flyer
b. Black PRies
c. Procter ' Gamble
d. Convergent

19. _________ is a branch of philosophy which seeks to address questions about morality, such as how a moral outcome can be achieved in a specific situation (applied _________), how moral values should be determined (normative _________), what moral values people actually abide by (descriptive _________), what the fundamental semantic, ontological, and epistemic nature of _________ or morality is (meta-_________), and how moral capacity or moral agency develops and what its nature is (moral psychology.)

Socrates was one of the first Greek philosophers to encourage both scholars and the common citizen to turn their attention from the outside world to the condition of man. In this view, Knowledge having a bearing on human life was placed highest, all other knowledge being secondary.

a. ADTECH
b. AMAX
c. Ethics
d. ACNielsen

20. Competitiveness is a comparative concept of the ability and performance of a firm, sub-sector or country to sell and supply goods and/or services in a given market. Although widely used in economics and business management, the usefulness of the concept, particularly in the context of national competitiveness, is vigorously disputed by economists, such as Paul Krugman .

The term may also be applied to markets, where it is used to refer to the extent to which the market structure may be regarded as perfectly _________.

a. Free trade zone
b. Geographical pricing
c. Customs union
d. Competitive

21. Consumer market research is a form of applied sociology that concentrates on understanding the behaviours, whims and preferences, of consumers in a market-based economy, and aims to understand the effects and comparative success of marketing campaigns. The field of consumer _________ as a statistical science was pioneered by Arthur Nielsen with the founding of the ACNielsen Company in 1923 .

Thus _________ is the systematic and objective identification, collection, analysis, and dissemination of information for the purpose of assisting management in decision making related to the identification and solution of problems and opportunities in marketing.

a. Marketing research
b. Marketing research process
c. Logit analysis
d. Focus group

22. A _________, in the field of business and marketing, is a geographic region or demographic group used to gauge the viability of a product or service in the mass market prior to a wide scale roll-out. The criteria used to judge the acceptability of a _________ region or group include:

1. a population that is demographically similar to the proposed target market; and
2. relative isolation from densely populated media markets so that advertising to the test audience can be efficient and economical.

The _________ ideally aims to duplicate 'everything' - promotion and distribution as well as `product' - on a smaller scale. The technique replicates, typically in one area, what is planned to occur in a national launch; and the results are very carefully monitored, so that they can be extrapolated to projected national results. The `area' may be any one of the following:

- Television area
- Test town
- Residential neighborhood
- Test site

A number of decisions have to be taken about any _________:

- Which _________?
- What is to be tested?
- How long a test?
- What are the success criteria?

The simple go or no-go decision, together with the related reduction of risk, is normally the main justification for the expense of _________s. At the same time, however, such _________s can be used to test specific elements of a new product's marketing mix; possibly the version of the product itself, the promotional message and media spend, the distribution channels and the price.

a. 180SearchAssistant
b. Preadolescence
c. Test market
d. Power III

23. A _________ is a plan of action designed to achieve a particular goal.

_________ is different from tactics. In military terms, tactics is concerned with the conduct of an engagement while _________ is concerned with how different engagements are linked.

a. Power III
b. 180SearchAssistant
c. 6-3-5 Brainwriting
d. Strategy

24. Advertising mail junk mail is the delivery of advertising material to recipients of postal mail. The delivery of advertising mail forms a large and growing service for many postal services, and _________ marketing forms a significant portion of the direct marketing industry. Some organizations attempt to help people opt-out of receiving advertising mail, in many cases motivated by a concern over its negative environmental impact.

a. Direct mail
b. Telemarketing
c. Directory Harvest Attack
d. Phishing

25. In mathematics, an _________, or central tendency of a data set refers to a measure of the 'middle' or 'expected' value of the data set. There are many different descriptive statistics that can be chosen as a measurement of the central tendency of the data items.

An _________ is a single value that is meant to typify a list of values.

a. ADTECH
b. AMAX
c. ACNielsen
d. Average

26. In economics, business, retail, and accounting, a _________ is the value of money that has been used up to produce something, and hence is not available for use anymore. In economics, a _________ is an alternative that is given up as a result of a decision. In business, the _________ may be one of acquisition, in which case the amount of money expended to acquire it is counted as _________.

a. Fixed costs
b. Transaction cost
c. Variable cost
d. Cost

27. The business terms _________ and pull originated in the logistic and supply chain management, but are also widely used in marketing.

A _________-pull-system in business describes the move of a product or information between two subjects. On markets the consumers usually 'pulls' the goods or information they demand for their needs, while the offerers or suppliers '_________es' them toward the consumers.

a. Gold Key Matching Service
b. Completely randomized designs
c. Manufacturers' representatives
d. Push

28. A _________ is a process that can allow an organization to concentrate its limited resources on the greatest opportunities to increase sales and achieve a sustainable competitive advantage. A _________ should be centered around the key concept that customer satisfaction is the main goal.

A _________ is most effective when it is an integral component of corporate strategy, defining how the organization will successfully engage customers, prospects, and competitors in the market arena.

a. Societal marketing
b. Marketing strategy
c. Cyberdoc
d. Psychographic

29. _________ is an advertisement in which a particular product specifically mentions a competitor by name for the express purpose of showing why the competitor is inferior to the product naming it.

This should not be confused with parody advertisements, where a fictional product is being advertised for the purpose of poking fun at the particular advertisement, nor should it be confused with the use of a coined brand name for the purpose of comparing the product without actually naming an actual competitor. ('Wikipedia tastes better and is less filling than the Encyclopedia Galactica.')

In the 1980s, during what has been referred to as the cola wars, soft-drink manufacturer Pepsi ran a series of advertisements where people, caught on hidden camera, in a blind taste test, chose Pepsi over rival Coca-Cola.

a. Comparative advertising
b. Heavy-up
c. Cost per conversion
d. GL-70

30. _________ is systematic determination of merit, worth, and significance of something or someone using criteria against a set of standards. _________ often is used to characterize and appraise subjects of interest in a wide range of human enterprises, including the arts, criminal justice, foundations and non-profit organizations, government, health care, and other human services.

Depending on the topic of interest, there are professional groups which look to the quality and rigor of the _________ process.

a. AMAX
b. ACNielsen
c. ADTECH
d. Evaluation

31. In marketing a _________ is a ticket or document that can be exchanged for a financial discount or rebate when purchasing a product. Customarily, _________s are issued by manufacturers of consumer packaged goods or by retailers, to be used in retail stores as a part of sales promotions. They are often widely distributed through mail, magazines, newspapers, the Internet, and mobile devices such as cell phones.

a. Merchandise
b. Merchandising
c. Coupon
d. Marketing communication

32. _________ in economics and business is the result of an exchange and from that trade we assign a numerical monetary value to a good, service or asset. If I trade 4 apples for an orange, the _________ of an orange is 4 - apples. Inversely, the _________ of an apple is 1/4 oranges.

a. Pricing
b. Discounts and allowances
c. Contribution margin-based pricing
d. Price

33. A _________ is an amount paid by way of reduction, return, or refund on what has already been paid or contributed. It is a type of sales promotion marketers use primarily as incentives or supplements to product sales. The mail-in _________ is the most common.

a. Lifestyle city
b. Strand
c. Personalization
d. Rebate

34. _________ is that part of statistical practice concerned with the selection of individual observations intended to yield some knowledge about a population of concern, especially for the purposes of statistical inference. Each observation measures one or more properties (weight, location, etc.) of an observable entity enumerated to distinguish objects or individuals.

a. AStore
b. Richard Buckminster 'Bucky' Fuller
c. Sports Marketing Group
d. Sampling

35. In the United States consumer sales promotions known as _________ or simply sweeps (both single and plural) have become associated with marketing promotions targeted toward both generating enthusiasm and providing incentive reactions among customers by enticing consumers to submit free entries into drawings of chance (and not skill) that are tied to product or service awareness wherein the featured prizes are given away by sponsoring companies. Prizes can vary in value from less than one dollar to more than one million U.S. dollars and can be in the form of cash, cars, homes, electronics, etc.

_________ frequently have eligibility limited by international, national, state, local, or other geographical factors.

a. Claritas Prizm
b. Commercial planning
c. Sweepstakes
d. Market segment

36. _________, also referred to as i-marketing, web marketing, online marketing is the marketing of products or services over the Internet.

The Internet has brought many unique benefits to marketing, one of which being lower costs for the distribution of information and media to a global audience. The interactive nature of _________, both in terms of providing instant response and eliciting responses, is a unique quality of the medium.

a. ACNielsen
b. Internet marketing
c. AMAX
d. ADTECH

37. A _________ is a single page leaflet advertising a nightclub, event, service, or other activity. _________s are typically used by individuals or businesses to promote their products or services. They are a form of mass marketing or small scale, community communication.

a. Quantitative
b. Flyer
c. Just-In-Case
d. Consumption Map

38. A _________ or community service announcement (CSA) is a non-commercial advertisement broadcast on radio or television, ostensibly for the public interest. _________s are intended to modify public attitudes by raising awareness about specific issues.

The most common topics of _________s are health and safety.

a. 180SearchAssistant
b. Public service announcement
c. Power III
d. 6-3-5 Brainwriting

39. _________ is anything that is generally accepted as payment for goods and services and repayment of debts. The main uses of _________ are as a medium of exchange, a unit of account, and a store of value. Some authors explicitly require _________ to be a standard of deferred payment.

a. Leading indicator
b. Microeconomics
c. Law of supply
d. Money

40. The _________ is an independent agency of the United States government, created, directed, and empowered by Congressional statute , and with the majority of its commissioners appointed by the current President.

a. Federal Communications Commission
b. Power III
c. 6-3-5 Brainwriting
d. 180SearchAssistant

41. The _________ is an independent agency of the United States government, established in 1914 by the _________ Act. Its principal mission is the promotion of 'consumer protection' and the elimination and prevention of what regulators perceive to be harmfully 'anti-competitive' business practices, such as coercive monopoly.

The _________ Act was one of President Wilson's major acts against trusts.

a. 6-3-5 Brainwriting
b. Power III
c. 180SearchAssistant
d. Federal Trade Commission

42. The U.S. _________ is an agency of the United States Department of Health and Human Services and is responsible for regulating and supervising the safety of foods, dietary supplements, drugs, vaccines, biological medical products, blood products, medical devices, radiation-emitting devices, veterinary products, and cosmetics. The FDA also enforces section 361 of the Public Health Service Act and the associated regulations, including sanitation requirements on interstate travel as well as specific rules for control of disease on products ranging from pet turtles to semen donations for assisted reproductive medicine techniques.

The FDA is an agency within the United States Department of Health and Human Services responsible for protecting and promoting the nation's public health.

a. 6-3-5 Brainwriting
b. 180SearchAssistant
c. Food and Drug Administration
d. Power III

43. The _________ is the de facto national library of the United States and the research arm of the United States Congress. Located in three buildings in Washington, D.C., it is the largest library in the world by shelf space and holds the largest number of books. The head of the Library is the Librarian of Congress, currently James H. Billington.

a. Power III
b. 6-3-5 Brainwriting
c. 180SearchAssistant
d. Library of Congress

44. A _________ is a set of exclusive rights granted by a State to an inventor or his assignee for a limited period of time in exchange for a disclosure of an invention.

The procedure for granting _________s, the requirements placed on the _________ee and the extent of the exclusive rights vary widely between countries according to national laws and international agreements. Typically, however, a _________ application must include one or more claims defining the invention which must be new, inventive, and useful or industrially applicable.

a. Product liability
b. Foreign Corrupt Practices Act
c. Reasonable person standard
d. Patent

45. The U.S. _________ is an independent agency of the United States government which holds primary responsibility for enforcing the federal securities laws and regulating the securities industry, the nation's stock and options exchanges, and other electronic securities markets. The SEC was created by section 4 of the Securities Exchange Act of 1934 (now codified as 15 U.S.C. Â§ 78d and commonly referred to as the 1934 Act.)

a. Securities and Exchange Commission
b. 180SearchAssistant
c. Power III
d. 6-3-5 Brainwriting

46. _________ refers to 'controlling human or societal behaviour by rules or restrictions.' _________ can take many forms: legal restrictions promulgated by a government authority, self-_________, social _________, co-_________ and market _________. One can consider _________ as actions of conduct imposing sanctions (such as a fine.) This action of administrative law, or implementing regulatory law, may be contrasted with statutory or case law.

a. Non-conventional trademark
b. Rule of four
c. CAN-SPAM
d. Regulation

1. The Oxford University Press defines _________ as 'marketing on a worldwide scale reconciling or taking commercial advantage of global operational differences, similarities and opportunities in order to meet global objectives.' Oxford University Press' Glossary of Marketing Terms.

Here are three reasons for the shift from domestic to _________ as given by the authors of the textbook, _________ Management--3rd Edition by Masaaki Kotabe and Kristiaan Helsen, 2004.

One of the product categories in which global competition has been easy to track is in U.S. automotive sales.

a. Digital marketing
b. Diversity marketing
c. Guerrilla Marketing
d. Global marketing

2. _________ is an advertisement in which a particular product specifically mentions a competitor by name for the express purpose of showing why the competitor is inferior to the product naming it.

This should not be confused with parody advertisements, where a fictional product is being advertised for the purpose of poking fun at the particular advertisement, nor should it be confused with the use of a coined brand name for the purpose of comparing the product without actually naming an actual competitor. ('Wikipedia tastes better and is less filling than the Encyclopedia Galactica.')

In the 1980s, during what has been referred to as the cola wars, soft-drink manufacturer Pepsi ran a series of advertisements where people, caught on hidden camera, in a blind taste test, chose Pepsi over rival Coca-Cola.

a. Heavy-up
b. GL-70
c. Cost per conversion
d. Comparative advertising

3. _________ is defined by the American _________ Association as the activity, set of institutions, and processes for creating, communicating, delivering, and exchanging offerings that have value for customers, clients, partners, and society at large. The term developed from the original meaning which referred literally to going to market, as in shopping, or going to a market to sell goods or services.

_________ practice tends to be seen as a creative industry, which includes advertising, distribution and selling.

a. Product naming
b. Marketing myopia
c. Customer acquisition management
d. Marketing

4. _________, according to Cornish, 'the process of acquiring and analyzing information in order to understand the market (both existing and potential customers); to determine the current and future needs and preferences, attitudes and behavior of the market; and to assess changes in the business environment that may affect the size and nature of the market in the future.' ('Product', 1997, p147.)

This figure shows how the interaction between variables from producers, communication channels, and consumers vary the effectiveness of _________ which affects the performance of the sales of a new product. The product is central in a circle because it helps to direct what information is gathered and how.

a. Line extension
b. Brand parity
c. Co-branding
d. Market intelligence

5. _________ is a form of social influence. It is the process of guiding people toward the adoption of an idea, attitude, or action by rational and symbolic (though not always logical) means. It is strategy of problem-solving relying on 'appeals' rather than coercion.

a. Power III
b. 6-3-5 Brainwriting
c. Persuasion
d. 180SearchAssistant

6. _________ is the physical search for minerals, fossils, precious metals or mineral specimens, and is also known as fossicking.

_________ is synonymous in some ways with mineral exploration which is an organised, large scale and at least semi-scientific effort undertaken by mineral resource companies to find commercially viable ore deposits. To actually be considered a prospector you must become registered as a professional prospector.

a. 180SearchAssistant
b. 6-3-5 Brainwriting
c. Prospecting
d. Power III

7. Procter is a surname, and may also refer to:

- Bryan Waller Procter (pseud. Barry Cornwall), English poet
- Goodwin Procter, American law firm
- _________, consumer products multinational

.

a. Procter ' Gamble
b. Convergent
c. Black PRies
d. Flyer

8. _________ is a marketing term that refers to the creation or generation of prospective consumer interest or inquiry into a business' products or services. Leads can be generated for a variety of purposes - list building, e-newsletter list acquisition or for winning customers.

A lead is a sign-up for an advertiser offer that includes contact information and in some cases, demographic information.

a. Sales process
b. Lead generation
c. Sales management
d. Hit rate

9. _________ in organizations and public policy is both the organizational process of creating and maintaining a plan; and the psychological process of thinking about the activities required to create a desired goal on some scale. As such, it is a fundamental property of intelligent behavior. This thought process is essential to the creation and refinement of a plan, or integration of it with other plans, that is, it combines forecasting of developments with the preparation of scenarios of how to react to them.

a. Power III
b. 180SearchAssistant
c. 6-3-5 Brainwriting
d. Planning

10. _________ is a broad label that refers to any individuals or households that use goods and services generated within the economy. The concept of a _________ is used in different contexts, so that the usage and significance of the term may vary.

A _________ is a person who uses any product or service.

a. 180SearchAssistant
b. Power III
c. 6-3-5 Brainwriting
d. Consumer

11. In economic models, the _________ time frame assumes no fixed factors of production. Firms can enter or leave the marketplace, and the cost (and availability) of land, labor, raw materials, and capital goods can be assumed to vary. In contrast, in the short-run time frame, certain factors are assumed to be fixed, because there is not sufficient time for them to change.

a. Power III
b. 180SearchAssistant
c. Long-run
d. 6-3-5 Brainwriting

12. A _________ is a type of business entity in which partners (owners) share with each other the profits or losses of the business undertaking in which all have invested. _________s are often favored over corporations for taxation purposes, as the _________ structure does not generally incur a tax on profits before it is distributed to the partners (i.e. there is no dividend tax levied.) However, depending on the _________ structure and the jurisdiction in which it operates, owners of a _________ may be exposed to greater personal liability than they would as shareholders of a corporation.

a. Brand piracy
b. Partnership
c. Competition law
d. Fair Debt Collection Practices Act

13. _________, a business term, is a measure of how products and services supplied by a company meet or surpass customer expectation. It is seen as a key performance indicator within business and is part of the four perspectives of a Balanced Scorecard.

In a competitive marketplace where businesses compete for customers, _________ is seen as a key differentiator and increasingly has become a key element of business strategy.

a. Customer base
b. Psychological pricing
c. Supplier diversity
d. Customer satisfaction

14. _________ is the practice of individuals including commercial businesses, governments and institutions, facilitating the sale of their products or services to other companies or organizations that in turn resell them, use them as components in products or services they offer _________ is also called business-to-_________ for short. (Note that while marketing to government entities shares some of the same dynamics of organizational marketing, B2G Marketing is meaningfully different.)

a. Law of disruption
b. Mass marketing
c. Business marketing
d. Disruptive technology

15. _________ in economics refers to metrics and measures of output from production processes, per unit of input. Labor _________, for example, is typically measured as a ratio of output per labor-hour, an input. _________ may be conceived of as a metrics of the technical or engineering efficiency of production.

a. Power III
b. Value engineering
c. 180SearchAssistant
d. Productivity

16. _________ can be regarded as an outcome of mental processes (cognitive process) leading to the selection of a course of action among several alternatives. Every _________ process produces a final choice. The output can be an action or an opinion of choice.

a. Decision making
b. 180SearchAssistant
c. Power III
d. 6-3-5 Brainwriting

17. Importance of _________ is critical for any commercial organization. Expanding business is not possible without increasing sales volumes, and effective _________ goal is to organize sales team work in such a manner that ensures a growing flow of regular customers and increasing amount of sales.

The four phase-model of Management Process

1. Conception
2. Planning
3. Execution
4. Control

This model is cyclical, so it is a constant/continuous process.

===_________ is attainment of sales force goals in a effective ' efficient manner through planning, staffing, training, leading ' controlling organizational resources.

a. Sales process
b. Hit rate
c. Request for proposal
d. Sales management

18. _________ is the study of the Earth and its lands, features, inhabitants, and phenomena. A literal translation would be 'to describe or write about the Earth'. The first person to use the word '_________' was Eratosthenes .

a. 6-3-5 Brainwriting
b. 180SearchAssistant
c. Power III
d. Geography

19. In probability theory and statistics, _________ indicates the strength and direction of a linear relationship between two random variables. That is in contrast with the usage of the term in colloquial speech, denoting any relationship, not necessarily linear. In general statistical usage, _________ or co-relation refers to the departure of two random variables from independence.

a. Probability
b. Mean
c. Frequency distribution
d. Correlation

20. _________ is the imitation of some real thing, state of affairs, or process. The act of simulating something generally entails representing certain key characteristics or behaviors of a selected physical or abstract system.

_________ is used in many contexts, including the modeling of natural systems or human systems in order to gain insight into their functioning.

a. 6-3-5 Brainwriting
b. 180SearchAssistant
c. Power III
d. Simulation

21. A _________ is a list of the general tasks and responsibilities of a position. Typically, it also includes to whom the position reports, specifications such as the qualifications needed by the person in the job, salary range for the position, etc. A _________ is usually developed by conducting a job analysis, which includes examining the tasks and sequences of tasks necessary to perform the job.

a. Power III
b. Job description
c. 6-3-5 Brainwriting
d. 180SearchAssistant

22. _________ generally refers to a list of all planned expenses and revenues. It is a plan for saving and spending. A _________ is an important concept in microeconomics, which uses a _________ line to illustrate the trade-offs between two or more goods.

a. Power III
b. Budget
c. 6-3-5 Brainwriting
d. 180SearchAssistant

23. _________ is systematic determination of merit, worth, and significance of something or someone using criteria against a set of standards. _________ often is used to characterize and appraise subjects of interest in a wide range of human enterprises, including the arts, criminal justice, foundations and non-profit organizations, government, health care, and other human services.

Depending on the topic of interest, there are professional groups which look to the quality and rigor of the _________ process.

a. ACNielsen
b. ADTECH
c. AMAX
d. Evaluation

24. In accounting, _________ has a very specific meaning. It is an outflow of cash or other valuable assets from a person or company to another person or company. This outflow of cash is generally one side of a trade for products or services that have equal or better current or future value to the buyer than to the seller.

a. AMAX
b. ACNielsen
c. ADTECH
d. Expense

25. _________ describes the situation when output from (or information about the result of) an event or phenomenon in the past will influence the same event/phenomenon in the present or future. When an event is part of a chain of cause-and-effect that forms a circuit or loop, then the event is said to 'feed back' into itself.

_________ is also a synonym for:

- _________ Signal; the information about the initial event that is the basis for subsequent modification of the event.
- _________ Loop; the causal path that leads from the initial generation of the _________ signal to the subsequent modification of the event.

_________ is a mechanism, process or signal that is looped back to control a system within itself. Such a loop is called a _________ loop.

a. Feedback
b. 6-3-5 Brainwriting
c. Power III
d. 180SearchAssistant

26. In economics and sociology, an _________ is any factor (financial or non-financial) that enables or motivates a particular course of action, or counts as a reason for preferring one choice to the alternatives. It is an expectation that encourages people to behave in a certain way. Since human beings are purposeful creatures, the study of _________ structures is central to the study of all economic activity (both in terms of individual decision-making and in terms of co-operation and competition within a larger institutional structure.)

a. ACNielsen
b. AMAX
c. ADTECH
d. Incentive

27. _________ is the set of reasons that determines one to engage in a particular behavior. The term is generally used for human _________ but, theoretically, it can be used to describe the causes for animal behavior as well

a. Role playing
b. Power III
c. 180SearchAssistant
d. Motivation

28. _________, when used as a special term, refers to various incentive plans introduced by businesses that provide direct or indirect payments to employees that depend on company's profitability in addition to employees' regular salary and bonuses. In publicly traded companies these plans typically amount to allocation of shares to employees.

The _________ plans are based on predetermined economic sharing rules that define the split of gains between the company as a principal and the employee as an agent.

a. Power III
b. 180SearchAssistant
c. 6-3-5 Brainwriting
d. Profit sharing

29. In finance, an _________ is a contract between a buyer and a seller that gives the buyer the right--but not the obligation--to buy or to sell a particular asset (the underlying asset) at a later day at an agreed price. In return for granting the _________, the seller collects a payment (the premium) from the buyer. A call _________ gives the buyer the right to buy the underlying asset; a put _________ gives the buyer of the _________ the right to sell the underlying asset.

a. AMAX
b. ADTECH
c. ACNielsen
d. Option

30. A _________ is a brief statement of the purpose of a company, organization. It is ideally used to guide the actions of the organization.

_________s often contain the following:

- Purpose of the organization
- The organization's primary stakeholders: clients, stockholders, etc.
- Responsibilities of the organization towards these stockholders
- Products and services offered

Generally shorter _________s are more effective than longer ones.

In developing a _________:

- Encourage input as feasible from employees, volunteers, and other stakeholders
- Publicize it broadly

The _________ can be used to resolve differences between business stakeholders. Stakeholders include: employees including managers and executives, stockholders, board of directors, customers, suppliers, distributors, creditors, governments (local, state, federal, etc.), unions, competitors, NGO's, and the general public.

a. 180SearchAssistant
b. 6-3-5 Brainwriting
c. Mission statement
d. Power III

1. _________ is one of the four elements of marketing mix. An organization or set of organizations (go-betweens) involved in the process of making a product or service available for use or consumption by a consumer or business user.

The other three parts of the marketing mix are product, pricing, and promotion.

a. Distribution
b. Better Living Through Chemistry
c. Japan Advertising Photographers' Association
d. Comparison-Shopping agent

2. _________ is defined by the American _________ Association as the activity, set of institutions, and processes for creating, communicating, delivering, and exchanging offerings that have value for customers, clients, partners, and society at large. The term developed from the original meaning which referred literally to going to market, as in shopping, or going to a market to sell goods or services.

_________ practice tends to be seen as a creative industry, which includes advertising, distribution and selling.

a. Marketing
b. Marketing myopia
c. Customer acquisition management
d. Product naming

3. A _________ is a list of the general tasks and responsibilities of a position. Typically, it also includes to whom the position reports, specifications such as the qualifications needed by the person in the job, salary range for the position, etc. A _________ is usually developed by conducting a job analysis, which includes examining the tasks and sequences of tasks necessary to perform the job.

a. Power III
b. 6-3-5 Brainwriting
c. Job description
d. 180SearchAssistant

4. _________ in organizations and public policy is both the organizational process of creating and maintaining a plan; and the psychological process of thinking about the activities required to create a desired goal on some scale. As such, it is a fundamental property of intelligent behavior. This thought process is essential to the creation and refinement of a plan, or integration of it with other plans, that is, it combines forecasting of developments with the preparation of scenarios of how to react to them.

a. Power III
b. Planning
c. 6-3-5 Brainwriting
d. 180SearchAssistant

5. A _________ is a party that mediates between a buyer and a seller. A _________ who also acts as a seller or as a buyer becomes a principal party to the deal. Distinguish agent: one who acts on behalf of a principal.

a. Power III
b. 180SearchAssistant
c. Spokesperson
d. Broker

6. _________s function as professionals who deal with trade, dealing in commodities that they do not produce themselves, in order to produce profit.

_________s can be of two types:

1. A wholesale _________ operates in the chain between producer and retail _________. Some wholesale _________s only organize the movement of goods rather than move the goods themselves.
2. A retail _________ or retailer, sells commodities to consumers (including businesses.) A shop owner is a retail _________.

A _________ class characterizes many pre-modern societies. Its status can range from high (even achieving titles like that of _________ prince or nabob) to low, such as in Chinese culture, due to the soiling capabilities of profiting from 'mere' trade, rather than from the labor of others reflected in agricultural produce, craftsmanship, and tribute.

In the United States, '_________' is defined (under the Uniform Commercial Code) as any person while engaged in a business or profession or a seller who deals regularly in the type of goods sold.

a. Trade credit
b. Retail loss prevention
c. RFM
d. Merchant

7. _________ is a concept that denotes the precise probability of specific eventualities. Technically, the notion of _________ is independent from the notion of value and, as such, eventualities may have both beneficial and adverse consequences. However, in general usage the convention is to focus only on potential negative impact to some characteristic of value that may arise from a future event.

a. Power III
b. 6-3-5 Brainwriting
c. Risk
d. 180SearchAssistant

8. _________ is a broad label that refers to any individuals or households that use goods and services generated within the economy. The concept of a _________ is used in different contexts, so that the usage and significance of the term may vary.

A _________ is a person who uses any product or service.

a. 180SearchAssistant
b. Consumer
c. Power III
d. 6-3-5 Brainwriting

9. _________ are final goods specifically intended for the mass market. For instance, _________ do not include investment assets, like precious antiques, even though these antiques are final goods.

Manufactured goods are goods that have been processed by way of machinery.

a. Durable good
b. Consumer goods
c. Free good
d. Power III

10. _________ is a sub-discipline and type of marketing. There are two main definitional characteristics which distinguish it from other types of marketing. The first is that it attempts to send its messages directly to consumers, without the use of intervening media.

a. Database marketing
b. Power III
c. Direct Marketing Associations
d. Direct marketing

11. A _________ is a type of wholesale merchant business that buys goods and bulk products from importers, other wholesalers and then sells to retailers. _________s can deal in any commodity destined for the retail market. Typical categories are food, lumber, hardware, fuel, and textiles.

a. Chief privacy officer
b. Refusal to deal
c. Tacit collusion
d. Jobbing house

12. _________ is anything that is intended to save time, energy or frustration. A _________ store at a petrol station, for example, sells items that have nothing to do with gasoline/petrol, but it saves the consumer from having to go to a grocery store. '_________' is a very relative term and its meaning tends to change over time.

a. MaxDiff
b. Demographic profile
c. Marketing buzz
d. Convenience

13. _________ operations or facilities are commonly called 'distribution centers'. '_________' is the term generally used to describe the process or the work flow associated with the picking, packing and delivery of the packed item(s) to a shipping carrier.

a. AMAX
b. Order processing
c. ACNielsen
d. ADTECH

14. In economics, business, retail, and accounting, a _________ is the value of money that has been used up to produce something, and hence is not available for use anymore. In economics, a _________ is an alternative that is given up as a result of a decision. In business, the _________ may be one of acquisition, in which case the amount of money expended to acquire it is counted as _________.

a. Transaction cost
b. Fixed costs
c. Variable cost
d. Cost

15. _________ is a list for goods and materials held available in stock by a business. It is also used for a list of the contents of a household and for a list for testamentary purposes of the possessions of someone who has died. In accounting _________ is considered an asset.

a. Inventory
b. Ending Inventory
c. ACNielsen
d. ADTECH

16. _________ is a form of marketing developed from direct response marketing campaigns conducted in the 1970's and 1980's which emphasizes customer retention and satisfaction, rather than a dominant focus on 'point of sale' transactions.

_________ differs from other forms of marketing in that it recognizes the long term value to the firm of keeping customers, as opposed to direct or 'Intrusion' marketing, which focuses upon acquisition of new clients by targeting majority demographics based upon prospective client lists.

_________ refers to long-term and mutually beneficial arrangement wherein both buyer and seller focus on value enhancement through the certain of more satisfying exchange.This approach attempts to transcend the simple purchase exchange process with customer to make more meaningful and richer contact by providing a more holistic, personalized purchase, and use orn consumption experience to create stronger ties.

a. Global marketing
b. Guerrilla Marketing
c. Diversity marketing
d. Relationship marketing

17. In marketing, _________ refers to the total cost of holding inventory. This includes warehousing costs such as rent, utilities and salaries, financial costs such as opportunity cost, and inventory costs related to perishibility, shrinkage and insurance.

When there are no transaction costs for shipment, _________s are minimized when no excess inventory is held at all, as in a Just In Time production system.

a. Carrying cost
b. Merchandise management system
c. Vendor Managed Inventory
d. Reverse auction

18. The most important feature of a contract is that one party makes an _________ for an arrangement that another accepts. This can be called a 'concurrence of wills' or 'ad idem' (meeting of the minds) of two or more parties. The concept is somewhat contested.

a. ACNielsen
b. ADTECH
c. AMAX
d. Offer

19. _________ refers to the methods of practicing and using another person's philosophy of business. The franchisor grants the independent operator the right to distribute its products, techniques, and trademarks for a percentage of gross monthly sales and a royalty fee. Various tangibles and intangibles such as national or international advertising, training, and other support services are commonly made available by the franchisor.

a. Franchising
b. Power III
c. 180SearchAssistant
d. Franchise fee

20. A _________ is defined by the International Co-operative Alliance's Statement on the Co-operative Identity as an autonomous association of persons united voluntarily to meet their common economic, social, and cultural needs and aspirations through a jointly-owned and democratically-controlled enterprise. It is a business organization owned and operated by a group of individuals for their mutual benefit. A _________ may also be defined as a business owned and controlled equally by the people who use its services or who work at it.

a. 6-3-5 Brainwriting
b. Cooperative
c. 180SearchAssistant
d. Power III

21. _________, Gross profit margin or Gross Profit Rate can be defined as the amount of contribution to the business enterprise, after paying for direct-fixed and direct-variable unit costs, required to cover overheads (fixed commitments) and provide a buffer for unknown items. It expresses the relationship between gross profit and sales revenue.

It can be expressed in absolute terms:

Gross Profit = Revenue − Cost of Goods Sold

or as the ratio of gross profit to sales revenue, usually in the form of a percentage:

_________ Percentage = (Revenue-Cost of Goods Sold)/Revenue

Cost of goods sold includes variable costs and fixed costs directly linked to the product, such as material and labor.

a. 180SearchAssistant
b. Power III
c. Gross margin
d. Profit maximization

22. _________ refers to the additional value of a commodity over the cost of commodities used to produce it from the previous stage of production. An example is the price of gasoline at the pump over the price of the oil in it. In national accounts used in macroeconomics, it refers to the contribution of the factors of production, i.e., land, labor, and capital goods, to raising the value of a product and corresponds to the incomes received by the owners of these factors. The factors of production provide 'services' which raise the unit price of a product (X) relative to the cost per unit of intermediate goods used up in the production of X. _________ is shared between the factors of production (capital, labor, also human capital), giving rise to issues of distribution.

a. Power III
b. Value added
c. Deregulation
d. Consumer spending

23. In the technical language of the World Trade Organization (WTO) system, a _________ is used to restrain international trade in order to protect a certain home industry from foreign competition. A member may take a '_________' action (i.e., restrict importation of a product temporarily) to protect a specific domestic industry from an increase in imports of any product which is causing, or which is threatening to cause, serious injury to the domestic industry that produces like or directly-competitive products.

_________ measures were always available under the General Agreement on Tariffs and Trade (GATT) (Article XIX).

a. Customs union
b. Countervailing duties
c. Gray market
d. Safeguard

24. A personal and cultural _________ is a relative ethic _________, an assumption upon which implementation can be extrapolated. A _________ system is a set of consistent _________s and measures that is soo not true. A principle _________ is a foundation upon which other _________s and measures of integrity are based.

a. Package-on-Package
b. Value
c. Perceptual maps
d. Supreme Court of the United States

25. A _________ is a retail establishment which specializes in selling a wide range of products without a single predominant merchandise line. _________s usually sell products including apparel, furniture, appliances, electronics, and additionally select other lines of products such as paint, hardware, toiletries, cosmetics, photographic equipment, jewelery, toys, and sporting goods. Certain _________s are further classified as discount _________s.

a. Power III
b. 180SearchAssistant
c. 6-3-5 Brainwriting
d. Department store

26. A _________ is a type of department store, which sell products at prices lower than those asked by traditional retail outlets. Most discount department stores offer wide assortments of goods; others specialize in such merchandise as jewelry, electronic equipment, or electrical appliances. _________s are not dollar stores, which sell goods at a dollar or less.

a. Strip mall
b. Discount store
c. Gruen transfer
d. Sales per unit area

27. An _________ is the manufacturing of a good or service within a category. Although _________ is a broad term for any kind of economic production, in economics and urban planning _________ is a synonym for the secondary sector, which is a type of economic activity involved in the manufacturing of raw materials into goods and products.

There are four key industrial economic sectors: the primary sector, largely raw material extraction industries such as mining and farming; the secondary sector, involving refining, construction, and manufacturing; the tertiary sector, which deals with services (such as law and medicine) and distribution of manufactured goods; and the quaternary sector, a relatively new type of knowledge _________ focusing on technological research, design and development such as computer programming, and biochemistry.

a. ADTECH
b. AMAX
c. ACNielsen
d. Industry

28. _________ is a market coverage strategy in which a firm decides to ignore market segment differences and go after the whole market with one offer.it is type of marketing (or attempting to sell through persuasion) of a product to a wide audience. The idea is to broadcast a message that will reach the largest number of people possible. Traditionally _________ has focused on radio, television and newspapers as the medium used to reach this broad audience.

a. Mass marketing
b. Cyberdoc
c. Marketspace
d. Business-to-consumer

29. The _________ or _________ is used by business and government to classify and measure economic activity in Canada, Mexico and the United States. It has largely replaced the older Standard Industrial Classification system; however, certain government departments and agencies, such as the U.S. Securities and Exchange Commission (SEC), still use the SIC codes.

The _________ numbering system is a six-digit code.

a. 180SearchAssistant
b. Power III
c. 6-3-5 Brainwriting
d. North American Industry Classification System

30. A _________ is a commercial building for storage of goods. _________s are used by manufacturers, importers, exporters, wholesalers, transport businesses, customs, etc. They are usually large plain buildings in industrial areas of cities and towns.

a. 180SearchAssistant
b. Power III
c. 6-3-5 Brainwriting
d. Warehouse

31. A _________ is a retail store, usually selling a wide variety of merchandise, in which customers pay annual membership fees in order to shop. The clubs are able to keep prices low due to the no-frills format of the stores. In addition, customers are required to buy large, wholesale quantities of the store's products, which makes these clubs attractive to both bargain hunters and small business owners.

a. Consignment
b. Power centre
c. Self service
d. Warehouse club

32. A _________ is a small store or shop that sells candy, ice-cream, soft drinks, lottery tickets, newspapers and magazines, along with a small selection of food and grocery supplies. Stores that are part of gas stations may also sell motor oil, windshield washer fluid, radiator fluid, and maps. Often toiletries and other hygiene products are stocked, and some of these stores also offer money orders and wire transfer services or liquor products.

a. 180SearchAssistant
b. Convenience store
c. 6-3-5 Brainwriting
d. Power III

33. _________ consists of the sale of goods or merchandise from a fixed location, such as a department store or kiosk in small or individual lots for direct consumption by the purchaser. _________ may include subordinated services, such as delivery. Purchasers may be individuals or businesses.

a. Thrifting
b. Charity shop
c. Retailing
d. Warehouse store

34. _________ is a term used in marketing and strategic management to describe a product, service, brand, or company that has such a distinct sustainable competitive advantage that competing firms find it almost impossible to operate profitably in that industry. The existence of a _________ will eliminate almost all market entities, whether real or virtual. Many existing firms will leave the industry, thereby increasing the industry's concentration ratio.

a. Category killer
b. Power III
c. 180SearchAssistant
d. 6-3-5 Brainwriting

35. Advertising mail junk mail is the delivery of advertising material to recipients of postal mail. The delivery of advertising mail forms a large and growing service for many postal services, and _________ marketing forms a significant portion of the direct marketing industry. Some organizations attempt to help people opt-out of receiving advertising mail, in many cases motivated by a concern over its negative environmental impact.

a. Phishing
b. Direct mail
c. Telemarketing
d. Directory Harvest Attack

36. _________ are small stores which specialize in a specific range of merchandise and related items. Most stores have an extensive width and depth of stock in the item that they specify in and provide high levels of service and expertise. The pricing policy is generally in the medium to high range, depending on factors like the type and exclusivity of merchandise and ownership, that is, whether they are owner operated or a chain operation which has the advantage of bulk purchasing and centralized warehousing system.

a. Wardrobing
b. Catalog merchant
c. Specialty stores
d. Brick and mortar business

37. _________ is a term commonly used to describe commerce transactions between businesses like the one between a manufacturer and a wholesaler or a wholesaler and a retailer i.e both the buyer and the seller are business entity.This is unlike business-to-consumers (B2C) which involve a business entity and end consumer, or business-to-government (B2G) which involve a business entity and government.

The volume of B2B transactions is much higher than the volume of B2C transactions. The primary reason for this is that in a typical supply chain there will be many B2B transactions involving subcomponent or raw materials, and only one B2C transaction, specifically sale of the finished product to the end customer.

a. Social marketing
b. Customer relationship management
c. Business-to-business
d. Disruptive technology

38. _________ describes activities of businesses serving end consumers with products and/or services.

An example of a B2C transaction would be a person buying a pair of shoes from a retailer. The transactions that led to the shoes being available for purchase, that is the purchase of the leather, laces, rubber, etc.

a. Corporate capabilities package
b. Societal marketing
c. Demand generation
d. Business-to-consumer

39. _________ commonly refers to the electronic retailing / _________ channels industry, which includes such billion dollar companies as Home shoppingN, QVC, eBay, ShopNBC, Buy.com, and Amazon.com. _________ allows consumers to shop for goods while in the privacy of their own home, as opposed to traditional shopping, which requires you to visit brick and mortar stores and shopping malls.

The _________ / electronic retailing industry was created in 1977 when small market radio talk show host Bob Circosta was asked to sell avocado-green-colored can openers live on the air by station owner Bud Paxson when an advertiser traded 112 units of product instead of paying his advertising bill.

a. Power III
b. Home Shopping
c. 6-3-5 Brainwriting
d. 180SearchAssistant

40. _________, also referred to as i-marketing, web marketing, online marketing is the marketing of products or services over the Internet.

The Internet has brought many unique benefits to marketing, one of which being lower costs for the distribution of information and media to a global audience. The interactive nature of _________, both in terms of providing instant response and eliciting responses, is a unique quality of the medium.

a. AMAX
b. ADTECH
c. ACNielsen
d. Internet marketing

41. _________ is the examining of goods or services from retailers with the intent to purchase at that time. _________ is an activity of selection and/or purchase. In some contexts it is considered a leisure activity as well as an economic one.

a. Khodebshchik
b. Hawkers
c. Shopping
d. Discount store

42. Electronic commerce, commonly known as _________ or eCommerce, consists of the buying and selling of products or services over electronic systems such as the Internet and other computer networks. The amount of trade conducted electronically has grown extraordinarily with wide-spread Internet usage. A wide variety of commerce is conducted in this way, spurring and drawing on innovations in electronic funds transfer, supply chain management, Internet marketing, online transaction processing, electronic data interchange (EDI), inventory management systems, and automated data collection systems.

a. ADTECH
b. ACNielsen
c. AMAX
d. E-commerce

43. In economics and especially in the theory of competition, _________ are obstacles in the path of a firm that make it difficult to enter a given market.

_________ are the source of a firm's pricing power - the ability of a firm to raise prices without losing all its customers.

The term refers to hindrances that an individual may face while trying to gain entrance into a profession or trade.

a. Predatory pricing
b. 180SearchAssistant
c. Power III
d. Barriers to entry

1. In economics, _________ is the desire to own something and the ability to pay for it. The term _________ signifies the ability or the willingness to buy a particular commodity at a given point of time .

.

a. Demand
b. Discretionary spending
c. Market dominance
d. Market system

2. _________ or _________ data refers to selected population characteristics as used in government, marketing or opinion research, or the _________ profiles used in such research. Note the distinction from the term 'demography' Commonly-used _________ include race, age, income, disabilities, mobility (in terms of travel time to work or number of vehicles available), educational attainment, home ownership, employment status, and even location.

a. Albert Einstein
b. Demographic
c. African Americans
d. AStore

3. _________ is defined by the American _________ Association as the activity, set of institutions, and processes for creating, communicating, delivering, and exchanging offerings that have value for customers, clients, partners, and society at large. The term developed from the original meaning which referred literally to going to market, as in shopping, or going to a market to sell goods or services.

_________ practice tends to be seen as a creative industry, which includes advertising, distribution and selling.

a. Marketing myopia
b. Product naming
c. Customer acquisition management
d. Marketing

4. _________ is a business discipline which is focused on the practical application of marketing techniques and the management of a firm's marketing resources and activities. Marketing managers are often responsible for influencing the level, timing, and composition of customer demand accepted definition of the term. In part, this is because the role of a marketing manager can vary significantly based on a business' size, corporate culture, and industry context.

a. Performance-based advertising
b. Business structure
c. Door-to-door
d. Marketing management

5. _________ is one of the four Ps of the marketing mix. The other three aspects are product, promotion, and place. It is also a key variable in microeconomic price allocation theory.

a. Competitor indexing
b. Relationship based pricing
c. Price
d. Pricing

6. _________ refer to a collection of facts usually collected as the result of experience, observation or experiment or a set of premises. This may consist of numbers, words particularly as measurements or observations of a set of variables. _________ are often viewed as a lowest level of abstraction from which information and knowledge are derived.

a. Sample size
b. Data
c. Pearson product-moment correlation coefficient
d. Mean

7. _________ is a marketing strategy that involves offering several products for sale as one combined product. This strategy is very common in the software business (for example: bundle a word processor, a spreadsheet, and a database into a single office suite), in the cable television industry (for example, basic cable in the United States generally offers many channels at one price), and in the fast food industry in which multiple items are combined into a complete meal. A bundle of products is sometimes referred to as a package deal or a compilation or an anthology.

a. Psychographic
b. Primary research
c. Technology acceptance model
d. Product bundling

8. _________ is a broad label that refers to any individuals or households that use goods and services generated within the economy. The concept of a _________ is used in different contexts, so that the usage and significance of the term may vary.

A _________ is a person who uses any product or service.

a. 6-3-5 Brainwriting
b. Consumer
c. 180SearchAssistant
d. Power III

9. _________, also referred to as i-marketing, web marketing, online marketing is the marketing of products or services over the Internet.

The Internet has brought many unique benefits to marketing, one of which being lower costs for the distribution of information and media to a global audience. The interactive nature of _________, both in terms of providing instant response and eliciting responses, is a unique quality of the medium.

a. AMAX
b. ACNielsen
c. ADTECH
d. Internet marketing

10. _________ in economics and business is the result of an exchange and from that trade we assign a numerical monetary value to a good, service or asset. If I trade 4 apples for an orange, the _________ of an orange is 4 - apples. Inversely, the _________ of an apple is 1/4 oranges.

a. Pricing
b. Contribution margin-based pricing
c. Discounts and allowances
d. Price

11. _________ or price ending is a marketing practice based on the theory that certain prices have a psychological impact. The retail prices are often expressed as 'odd prices': a little less than a round number, e.g. $19.99 or Â£6.95 (but not necessarily mathematically odd, it could also be 2.98.) The theory is this drives demand greater than would be expected if consumers were perfectly rational.

a. Supplier diversity
b. Chain stores
c. Psychological pricing
d. First-mover advantage

12. _________ is a rivalry between individuals, groups, nations for territory, a niche, or allocation of resources. It arises whenever two or more parties strive for a goal which cannot be shared. _________ occurs naturally between living organisms which co-exist in the same environment.

a. Price fixing
b. Price competition
c. Competition
d. Non-price competition

13. In economics, _________ is the ratio of the percent change in one variable to the percent change in another variable. It is a tool for measuring the responsiveness of a function to changes in parameters in a relative way. Commonly analyzed are _________ of substitution, price and wealth.

a. ACNielsen
b. Opinion leadership
c. Elasticity
d. Intellectual property

14. In psychology, philosophy, and the cognitive sciences, _________ is the process of attaining awareness or understanding of sensory information. It is a task far more complex than was imagined in the 1950s and 1960s, when it was predicted that building perceiving machines would take about a decade, a goal which is still very far from fruition. The word _________ comes from the Latin words _________, percepio, meaning 'receiving, collecting, action of taking possession, apprehension with the mind or senses.'

_________ is one of the oldest fields in psychology.

a. Power III
b. Groupthink
c. 180SearchAssistant
d. Perception

15. The break-even point for a product is the point where total revenue received equals the total costs associated with the sale of the product (TR=TC.) A break-even point is typically calculated in order for businesses to determine if it would be profitable to sell a proposed product, as opposed to attempting to modify an existing product instead so it can be made lucrative. _________ can also be used to analyse the potential profitability of an expenditure in a sales-based business.

In _________, margin of safety is how much output or sales level can fall before a business reaches its break-even point (BEP).

a. Price skimming
b. Pay Per Sale
c. Contribution margin-based pricing
d. Break even analysis

16. _________ is a pricing method used by companies. It is used primarily because it is easy to calculate and requires little information. There are several varieties, but the common thread in all of them is that one first calculates the cost of the product, then includes an additional amount to represent profit.

a. Relationship based pricing
b. Break even analysis
c. Loss leader
d. Cost-plus pricing

17. _________ or goals give direction to the whole pricing process. Determining what your objectives are is the first step in pricing. When deciding on _________ you must consider: 1) the overall financial, marketing, and strategic objectives of the company; 2) the objectives of your product or brand; 3) consumer price elasticity and price points; and 4) the resources you have available.

a. Discounts and allowances
b. Transfer pricing
c. Competitor indexing
d. Pricing objectives

18. In economics, _________ is the process by which a firm determines the price and output level that returns the greatest profit. There are several approaches to this problem. The total revenue--total cost method relies on the fact that profit equals revenue minus cost, and the marginal revenue--marginal cost method is based on the fact that total profit in a perfectly competitive market reaches its maximum point where marginal revenue equals marginal cost.

a. Power III
b. 180SearchAssistant
c. Profit margin
d. Profit maximization

19. In economics, business, retail, and accounting, a _________ is the value of money that has been used up to produce something, and hence is not available for use anymore. In economics, a _________ is an alternative that is given up as a result of a decision. In business, the _________ may be one of acquisition, in which case the amount of money expended to acquire it is counted as _________.

a. Transaction cost
b. Variable cost
c. Cost
d. Fixed costs

20. _________ is a list for goods and materials held available in stock by a business. It is also used for a list of the contents of a household and for a list for testamentary purposes of the possessions of someone who has died. In accounting _________ is considered an asset.

a. Ending Inventory
b. ADTECH
c. ACNielsen
d. Inventory

21. An _________, operating expenditure, operational expense, operational expenditure or OPEX is an on-going cost for running a product, business, or system. Its counterpart, a capital expenditure (CAPEX), is the cost of developing or providing non-consumable parts for the product or system. For example, the purchase of a photocopier is the CAPEX, and the annual paper and toner cost is the OPEX.

a. AMAX
b. ADTECH
c. ACNielsen
d. Operating expense

22. _________ exists when sales of identical goods or services are transacted at different prices from the same provider. In a theoretical market with perfect information, no transaction costs or prohibition on secondary exchange (or re-selling) to prevent arbitrage, _________ can only be a feature of monopoly and oligopoly markets, where market power can be exercised. Otherwise, the moment the seller tries to sell the same good at different prices, the buyer at the lower price can arbitrage by selling to the consumer buying at the higher price but with a tiny discount.

a. Price
b. Penetration pricing
c. Resale price maintenance
d. Price discrimination

23. In accounting, _________ has a very specific meaning. It is an outflow of cash or other valuable assets from a person or company to another person or company. This outflow of cash is generally one side of a trade for products or services that have equal or better current or future value to the buyer than to the seller.

a. ADTECH
b. ACNielsen
c. AMAX
d. Expense

24. A _________ is a collection of symbols, experiences and associations connected with a product, a service, a person or any other artifact or entity.

_________s have become increasingly important components of culture and the economy, now being described as 'cultural accessories and personal philosophies'.

Some people distinguish the psychological aspect of a _________ from the experiential aspect.

a. Store brand
b. Brandable software
c. Brand equity
d. Brand

25. _________ refers to the marketing effects or outcomes that accrue to a product with its brand name compared with those that would accrue if the same product did not have the brand name . And, at the root of these marketing effects is consumers' knowledge. In other words, consumers' knowledge about a brand makes manufacturers/advertisers respond differently or adopt appropriately adapt measures for the marketing of the brand .

a. Brand image
b. Brand aversion
c. Brand equity
d. Product extension

26. Trademark _________ is an important concept in the law governing trademarks and service marks. A trademark may be eligible for registration, or registrable, if amongst other things it performs the essential trademark function, and has distinctive character. Registrability can be understood as a continuum, with 'inherently distinctive' marks at one end, 'generic' and 'descriptive' marks with no distinctive character at the other end, and 'suggestive' and 'arbitrary' marks lying between these two points.

a. Brand ambassador
b. Corporate colours
c. Brand implementation
d. Distinctiveness

27. _________ is the pricing technique of setting a relatively low initial entry price, often lower than the eventual market price, to attract new customers. The strategy works on the expectation that customers will switch to the new brand because of the lower price. _________ is most commonly associated with a marketing objective of increasing market share or sales volume, rather than to make profit in the short term.

a. Competitor indexing
b. Fee
c. Price war
d. Penetration pricing

28. _________ is used in marketing to describe the way in which service capacity cannot be stored for sale in the future. It is a key concept of services marketing.

Other key characteristics of services include intangibility, inseparability and variability.

a. Demonstrator model
b. Specialty catalogs
c. Perishability
d. National brand

29. _________ Management is the succession of strategies used by management as a product goes through its _________. The conditions in which a product is sold changes over time and must be managed as it moves through its succession of stages.

The _________ goes through many phases, involves many professional disciplines, and requires many skills, tools and processes.

a. Customer satisfaction
b. Chain stores
c. Supplier diversity
d. Product life cycle

30. The _________ is an independent agency of the United States government, established in 1914 by the _________ Act. Its principal mission is the promotion of 'consumer protection' and the elimination and prevention of what regulators perceive to be harmfully 'anti-competitive' business practices, such as coercive monopoly.

The _________ Act was one of President Wilson's major acts against trusts.

a. Power III
b. 180SearchAssistant
c. 6-3-5 Brainwriting
d. Federal Trade Commission

31. The _________ of 1914 (15 U.S.C Â§Â§ 41-58, as amended) established the Federal Trade Commission (FTC), a bipartisan body of five members appointed by the President of the United States for seven year terms. This Commission was authorized to issue Cease and Desist orders to large corporations to curb unfair trade practices. This Act also gave more flexibility to the US congress for judicial matters.

a. Gripe site
b. Comparative negligence
c. Federal Trade Commission Act
d. Product liability

32. _________ is an agreement between business competitors to sell the same product or service at the same price. In general, it is an agreement intended to ultimately push the price of a product as high as possible, leading to profits for all the sellers. _________ can also involve any agreement to fix, peg, discount or stabilize prices.

a. Price fixing
b. Direct competition
c. Non-price competition
d. Price competition

33. The _________ requires the Federal government to investigate and pursue trusts, companies and organizations suspected of violating the Act. It was the first United States Federal statute to limit cartels and monopolies, and today still forms the basis for most antitrust litigation by the federal government.

a. 6-3-5 Brainwriting
b. Sherman Antitrust Act
c. Power III
d. 180SearchAssistant

34. _________ is a form of communication that typically attempts to persuade potential customers to purchase or to consume more of a particular brand of product or service. 'While now central to the contemporary global economy and the reproduction of global production networks, it is only quite recently that _________ has been more than a marginal influence on patterns of sales and production. The formation of modern _________ was intimately bound up with the emergence of new forms of monopoly capitalism around the end of the 19th and beginning of the 20th century as one element in corporate strategies to create, organize and where possible control markets, especially for mass produced consumer goods.

a. ADTECH
b. AMAX
c. ACNielsen
d. Advertising

35. _________ refers to 'controlling human or societal behaviour by rules or restrictions.' _________ can take many forms: legal restrictions promulgated by a government authority, self-_________, social _________, co-_________ and market _________. One can consider _________ as actions of conduct imposing sanctions (such as a fine.) This action of administrative law, or implementing regulatory law, may be contrasted with statutory or case law.

a. Rule of four
b. Non-conventional trademark
c. CAN-SPAM
d. Regulation

36. The _________ of 1936 (or Anti-Price Discrimination Act, 15 U.S.C. Â§ 13) is a United States federal law that prohibits what were considered, at the time of passage, to be anticompetitive practices by producers, specifically price discrimination. It grew out of practices in which chain stores were allowed to purchase goods at lower prices than other retailers.

a. Registered trademark symbol
b. Trademark infringement
c. Fair Debt Collection Practices Act
d. Robinson-Patman Act

37. A personal and cultural _________ is a relative ethic _________, an assumption upon which implementation can be extrapolated. A _________ system is a set of consistent _________s and measures that is soo not true. A principle _________ is a foundation upon which other _________s and measures of integrity are based.

a. Package-on-Package
b. Value
c. Supreme Court of the United States
d. Perceptual maps

38. _________ is systematic determination of merit, worth, and significance of something or someone using criteria against a set of standards. _________ often is used to characterize and appraise subjects of interest in a wide range of human enterprises, including the arts, criminal justice, foundations and non-profit organizations, government, health care, and other human services.

Depending on the topic of interest, there are professional groups which look to the quality and rigor of the _________ process.

a. AMAX
b. ACNielsen
c. ADTECH
d. Evaluation

39. _________ commonly refers to the electronic retailing / _________ channels industry, which includes such billion dollar companies as Home shoppingN, QVC, eBay, ShopNBC, Buy.com, and Amazon.com. _________ allows consumers to shop for goods while in the privacy of their own home, as opposed to traditional shopping, which requires you to visit brick and mortar stores and shopping malls.

The _________ / electronic retailing industry was created in 1977 when small market radio talk show host Bob Circosta was asked to sell avocado-green-colored can openers live on the air by station owner Bud Paxson when an advertiser traded 112 units of product instead of paying his advertising bill.

a. Home shopping
b. Power III
c. 6-3-5 Brainwriting
d. 180SearchAssistant

40. The principle of _________ is the legal ideal that requires all law to be clear, ascertainable and non-retrospective. It requires decision makers to resolve disputes by applying legal rules that have been declared beforehand, and not to alter the legal situation retrospectively by discretionary departures from established law. It is closely related to legal formalism and the rule of law and can be traced from the writings of Feuerbach, Dicey and Montesquieu.

a. Power III
b. Legality
c. 180SearchAssistant
d. 6-3-5 Brainwriting

41. _________ is the examining of goods or services from retailers with the intent to purchase at that time. _________ is an activity of selection and/or purchase. In some contexts it is considered a leisure activity as well as an economic one.

a. Khodebshchik
b. Hawkers
c. Discount store
d. Shopping

42. In descriptive statistics, the _________ is the length of the smallest interval which contains all the data. It is calculated by subtracting the smallest observation (sample minimum) from the greatest (sample maximum) and provides an indication of statistical dispersion.

It is measured in the same units as the data.

a. Japan Advertising Photographers' Association
b. Personalization
c. Just-In-Case
d. Range

43. A _________ is a plan of action designed to achieve a particular goal.

_________ is different from tactics. In military terms, tactics is concerned with the conduct of an engagement while _________ is concerned with how different engagements are linked.

a. Power III
b. 180SearchAssistant
c. 6-3-5 Brainwriting
d. Strategy

1. The _________ is a professional association for marketers. As of 2008 it had approximately 40,000 members. There are collegiate chapters on 250 campuses.

a. AMAX
b. ADTECH
c. American Marketing Association
d. ACNielsen

2. _________ is a branch of philosophy which seeks to address questions about morality, such as how a moral outcome can be achieved in a specific situation (applied _________), how moral values should be determined (normative _________), what moral values people actually abide by (descriptive _________), what the fundamental semantic, ontological, and epistemic nature of _________ or morality is (meta-_________), and how moral capacity or moral agency develops and what its nature is (moral psychology.)

Socrates was one of the first Greek philosophers to encourage both scholars and the common citizen to turn their attention from the outside world to the condition of man. In this view, Knowledge having a bearing on human life was placed highest, all other knowledge being secondary.

a. ADTECH
b. ACNielsen
c. AMAX
d. Ethics

3. A variety of measures of national income and output are used in economics to estimate total economic activity in a country or region, including gross domestic product (GDP), _________ , and net national income (NNI).

_________ is defined as the 'value of all goods and services produced in a country in one year, plus income earned by its citizens abroad, minus income earned by foreigners in the country'.

a. Gross national product
b. Power III
c. Consumer Expenditure Survey
d. Bureau of Labor Statistics

4. _________ is defined by the American _________ Association as the activity, set of institutions, and processes for creating, communicating, delivering, and exchanging offerings that have value for customers, clients, partners, and society at large. The term developed from the original meaning which referred literally to going to market, as in shopping, or going to a market to sell goods or services.

_________ practice tends to be seen as a creative industry, which includes advertising, distribution and selling.

a. Product naming
b. Marketing myopia
c. Customer acquisition management
d. Marketing

5. The _________ is generally accepted as the use and specification of the four p's describing the strategic position of a product in the marketplace. One version of the origins of the _________ starts in 1948 when James Culliton said that a marketing decision should be a result of something similar to a recipe. This version continued in 1953 when Neil Borden, in his American Marketing Association presidential address, took the recipe idea one step further and coined the term 'Marketing-Mix'.

a. Marketing mix
b. 180SearchAssistant
c. 6-3-5 Brainwriting
d. Power III

6. _________ is an advertisement in which a particular product specifically mentions a competitor by name for the express purpose of showing why the competitor is inferior to the product naming it.

This should not be confused with parody advertisements, where a fictional product is being advertised for the purpose of poking fun at the particular advertisement, nor should it be confused with the use of a coined brand name for the purpose of comparing the product without actually naming an actual competitor. ('Wikipedia tastes better and is less filling than the Encyclopedia Galactica.')

In the 1980s, during what has been referred to as the cola wars, soft-drink manufacturer Pepsi ran a series of advertisements where people, caught on hidden camera, in a blind taste test, chose Pepsi over rival Coca-Cola.

a. Heavy-up
b. GL-70
c. Cost per conversion
d. Comparative advertising

7. A _________ is a type of wholesale merchant business that buys goods and bulk products from importers, other wholesalers and then sells to retailers. _________s can deal in any commodity destined for the retail market. Typical categories are food, lumber, hardware, fuel, and textiles.

a. Refusal to deal
b. Tacit collusion
c. Chief privacy officer
d. Jobbing house

8. _________ is used in marketing to describe the inability to assess the value gained from engaging in an activity using any tangible evidence. It is often used to describe services where there isn't a tangible product that the customer can purchase, that can be seen, tasted or touched.

Other key characteristics of services include perishability, inseparability and variability.

a. Automated surveys
b. Individual branding
c. Inseparability
d. Intangibility

9. _________ is one of the four elements of marketing mix. An organization or set of organizations (go-betweens) involved in the process of making a product or service available for use or consumption by a consumer or business user.

The other three parts of the marketing mix are product, pricing, and promotion.

a. Better Living Through Chemistry
b. Comparison-Shopping agent
c. Japan Advertising Photographers' Association
d. Distribution

10. _________s or 'eServices' is a highly general/generic term usually referring to the provision of services via the Internet (the prefix 'e' standing for 'electronic', as it does in many other uses.) It is true Web jargon, meaning just about anything done online. This page, for example, is an _________.

a. AMAX
b. ADTECH
c. ACNielsen
d. E-service

11. _________ is used in marketing to describe a key quality of services as distinct from goods. _________ is the characteristic that a service has which renders it impossible to divorce the supply or production of the service from its consumption.

Other key characteristics of services include perishability, intangibility and variability.

a. Individual branding
b. Inseparability
c. Engagement
d. Online focus group

12. _________ is a sub-discipline and type of marketing. There are two main definitional characteristics which distinguish it from other types of marketing. The first is that it attempts to send its messages directly to consumers, without the use of intervening media.

a. Direct Marketing Associations
b. Database marketing
c. Power III
d. Direct marketing

13. In economics, _________ is the desire to own something and the ability to pay for it. The term _________ signifies the ability or the willingness to buy a particular commodity at a given point of time .

.

a. Market dominance
b. Discretionary spending
c. Demand
d. Market system

14. _________, also referred to as i-marketing, web marketing, online marketing is the marketing of products or services over the Internet.

The Internet has brought many unique benefits to marketing, one of which being lower costs for the distribution of information and media to a global audience. The interactive nature of _________, both in terms of providing instant response and eliciting responses, is a unique quality of the medium.

a. AMAX
b. ADTECH
c. Internet marketing
d. ACNielsen

15. _________ is used in marketing to describe the way in which service capacity cannot be stored for sale in the future. It is a key concept of services marketing.

Other key characteristics of services include intangibility, inseparability and variability.

a. Specialty catalogs
b. National brand
c. Perishability
d. Demonstrator model

16. _________ in economics and business is the result of an exchange and from that trade we assign a numerical monetary value to a good, service or asset. If I trade 4 apples for an orange, the _________ of an orange is 4 - apples. Inversely, the _________ of an apple is 1/4 oranges.

a. Pricing
b. Contribution margin-based pricing
c. Discounts and allowances
d. Price

17. _________ exists when sales of identical goods or services are transacted at different prices from the same provider. In a theoretical market with perfect information, no transaction costs or prohibition on secondary exchange (or re-selling) to prevent arbitrage, _________ can only be a feature of monopoly and oligopoly markets, where market power can be exercised. Otherwise, the moment the seller tries to sell the same good at different prices, the buyer at the lower price can arbitrage by selling to the consumer buying at the higher price but with a tiny discount.

a. Penetration pricing
b. Price
c. Price discrimination
d. Resale price maintenance

18. In economics, _________ is the ratio of the percent change in one variable to the percent change in another variable. It is a tool for measuring the responsiveness of a function to changes in parameters in a relative way. Commonly analyzed are _________ of substitution, price and wealth.

a. Intellectual property
b. Elasticity
c. Opinion leadership
d. ACNielsen

19. An _________ is the manufacturing of a good or service within a category. Although _________ is a broad term for any kind of economic production, in economics and urban planning _________ is a synonym for the secondary sector, which is a type of economic activity involved in the manufacturing of raw materials into goods and products.

There are four key industrial economic sectors: the primary sector, largely raw material extraction industries such as mining and farming; the secondary sector, involving refining, construction, and manufacturing; the tertiary sector, which deals with services (such as law and medicine) and distribution of manufactured goods; and the quaternary sector, a relatively new type of knowledge _________ focusing on technological research, design and development such as computer programming, and biochemistry.

a. ADTECH
b. ACNielsen
c. Industry
d. AMAX

20. _________ is one of the four Ps of the marketing mix. The other three aspects are product, promotion, and place. It is also a key variable in microeconomic price allocation theory.

a. Relationship based pricing
b. Price
c. Competitor indexing
d. Pricing

21. In algebra, a _________ is a function depending on n that associates a scalar, det(A), to an n×n square matrix A. The fundamental geometric meaning of a _________ is a scale factor for measure when A is regarded as a linear transformation. _________s are important both in calculus, where they enter the substitution rule for several variables, and in multilinear algebra.

For a fixed nonnegative integer n, there is a unique _________ function for the n×n matrices over any commutative ring R. In particular, this function exists when R is the field of real or complex numbers.

a. Motion Picture Association of America's film-rating system
b. Determinant
c. Black Friday
d. Package-on-Package

22. In psychology, philosophy, and the cognitive sciences, _________ is the process of attaining awareness or understanding of sensory information. It is a task far more complex than was imagined in the 1950s and 1960s, when it was predicted that building perceiving machines would take about a decade, a goal which is still very far from fruition. The word _________ comes from the Latin words _________, percepio, meaning 'receiving, collecting, action of taking possession, apprehension with the mind or senses.'

_________ is one of the oldest fields in psychology.

a. Perception
b. Power III
c. Groupthink
d. 180SearchAssistant

23. _________ is an ongoing process that occurs strictly within a company or organization whereby the functional process aligns, motivates and empowers employees at all management levels to consistently deliver a satisfying customer experience. According to Burkitt and Zealley, 'the challenge for _________ is not only to get the right messages across, but to embed them in such a way that they both change and reinforce employee behaviour'.

a. AMAX
b. ACNielsen
c. Internal marketing
d. ADTECH

24. _________, a business term, is a measure of how products and services supplied by a company meet or surpass customer expectation. It is seen as a key performance indicator within business and is part of the four perspectives of a Balanced Scorecard.

In a competitive marketplace where businesses compete for customers, _________ is seen as a key differentiator and increasingly has become a key element of business strategy.

a. Supplier diversity
b. Customer base
c. Psychological pricing
d. Customer satisfaction

25. _________ is a contract between two parties, one being the employer and the other being the employee. An employee may be defined as: 'A person in the service of another under any contract of hire, express or implied, oral or written, where the employer has the power or right to control and direct the employee in the material details of how the work is to be performed.' Black's Law Dictionary page 471 (5th ed. 1979.)

a. ACNielsen
b. AMAX
c. ADTECH
d. Employment

26. _________ is a broad label that refers to any individuals or households that use goods and services generated within the economy. The concept of a _________ is used in different contexts, so that the usage and significance of the term may vary.

A _________ is a person who uses any product or service.

a. 6-3-5 Brainwriting
b. 180SearchAssistant
c. Power III
d. Consumer

27. _________ is the study of when, why, how, where and what people do or do not buy products. It blends elements from psychology, sociology,social psychology, anthropology and economics. It attempts to understand the buyer decision making process, both individually and in groups. It studies characteristics of individual consumers such as demographics and behavioural variables in an attempt to understand people's wants. It also tries to assess influences on the consumer from groups such as family, friends, reference groups, and society in general.

a. Consumer confidence
b. Multidimensional scaling
c. Communal marketing
d. Consumer behavior

28. A _________ is a plan of action designed to achieve a particular goal.

_________ is different from tactics. In military terms, tactics is concerned with the conduct of an engagement while _________ is concerned with how different engagements are linked.

a. 180SearchAssistant
b. Power III
c. Strategy
d. 6-3-5 Brainwriting

29. _________ is a rivalry between individuals, groups, nations for territory, a niche, or allocation of resources. It arises whenever two or more parties strive for a goal which cannot be shared. _________ occurs naturally between living organisms which co-exist in the same environment.

a. Non-price competition
b. Price competition
c. Price fixing
d. Competition

30. The Oxford University Press defines _________ as 'marketing on a worldwide scale reconciling or taking commercial advantage of global operational differences, similarities and opportunities in order to meet global objectives.' Oxford University Press' Glossary of Marketing Terms.

Here are three reasons for the shift from domestic to _________ as given by the authors of the textbook, _________ Management--3rd Edition by Masaaki Kotabe and Kristiaan Helsen, 2004.

One of the product categories in which global competition has been easy to track is in U.S. automotive sales.

a. Guerrilla Marketing
b. Diversity marketing
c. Digital marketing
d. Global marketing

31. _________ is a process by which government's control over businesses and individuals is reduced or eliminated. It is the removal of some governmental controls over a market. _________ does not mean elimination of laws against fraud, but eliminating or reducing government control of how business is done, thereby moving toward a more free market.

a. Power III
b. Consumer spending
c. Value added
d. Deregulation

32. _________ is marketing based on relationship and value. It may be used to market a service or a product.

Marketing a service-base business is different from marketing a goods-base business.

a. Power III
b. 6-3-5 Brainwriting
c. 180SearchAssistant
d. Services Marketing

33. _________ is the practice of individuals including commercial businesses, governments and institutions, facilitating the sale of their products or services to other companies or organizations that in turn resell them, use them as components in products or services they offer _________ is also called business-to-_________ for short. (Note that while marketing to government entities shares some of the same dynamics of organizational marketing, B2G Marketing is meaningfully different.)

a. Disruptive technology
b. Mass marketing
c. Law of disruption
d. Business marketing

34. _________ is the process of understanding, anticipating and influencing consumer behavior in order to maximize revenue or profits from a fixed, perishable resource This process was first discovered by Dr. Matt H. Keller. The challenge is to sell the right resources to the right customer at the right time for the right price. This process can result in price discrimination, where a firm charges customers consuming otherwise identical goods or services a different price for doing so.

a. Service provider
b. Yield management
c. Multi-level marketing
d. Cross-selling

35. _________ in organizations and public policy is both the organizational process of creating and maintaining a plan; and the psychological process of thinking about the activities required to create a desired goal on some scale. As such, it is a fundamental property of intelligent behavior. This thought process is essential to the creation and refinement of a plan, or integration of it with other plans, that is, it combines forecasting of developments with the preparation of scenarios of how to react to them.

a. 6-3-5 Brainwriting
b. 180SearchAssistant
c. Power III
d. Planning

1. _________ is a measure of the strength of a brand, product, service relative to competitive offerings. There is often a geographic element to the competitive landscape. In defining _________, you must see to what extent a product, brand, or firm controls a product category in a given geographic area.

a. Productivity
b. Discretionary spending
c. Market system
d. Market dominance

2. The Oxford University Press defines _________ as 'marketing on a worldwide scale reconciling or taking commercial advantage of global operational differences, similarities and opportunities in order to meet global objectives.' Oxford University Press' Glossary of Marketing Terms.

Here are three reasons for the shift from domestic to _________ as given by the authors of the textbook, _________ Management--3rd Edition by Masaaki Kotabe and Kristiaan Helsen, 2004.

One of the product categories in which global competition has been easy to track is in U.S. automotive sales.

a. Diversity marketing
b. Digital marketing
c. Guerrilla Marketing
d. Global marketing

3. A _________ or transnational corporation is a corporation or enterprise that manages production or delivers services in more than one country. It can also be referred to as an international corporation.

The first modern MNC is generally thought to be the British East India Company, established in 1600.

a. Hechsher
b. Checkoff
c. HD share
d. Multinational corporation

4. _________ is a fee paid on borrowed assets. It is the price paid for the use of borrowed money , or, money earned by deposited funds . Assets that are sometimes lent with _________ include money, shares, consumer goods through hire purchase, major assets such as aircraft, and even entire factories in finance lease arrangements.

a. AMAX
b. ACNielsen
c. ADTECH
d. Interest

5. _________ is defined by the American _________ Association as the activity, set of institutions, and processes for creating, communicating, delivering, and exchanging offerings that have value for customers, clients, partners, and society at large. The term developed from the original meaning which referred literally to going to market, as in shopping, or going to a market to sell goods or services.

_________ practice tends to be seen as a creative industry, which includes advertising, distribution and selling.

a. Product naming
b. Marketing
c. Customer acquisition management
d. Marketing myopia

6. Competitiveness is a comparative concept of the ability and performance of a firm, sub-sector or country to sell and supply goods and/or services in a given market. Although widely used in economics and business management, the usefulness of the concept, particularly in the context of national competitiveness, is vigorously disputed by economists, such as Paul Krugman .

The term may also be applied to markets, where it is used to refer to the extent to which the market structure may be regarded as perfectly _________.

a. Customs union
b. Geographical pricing
c. Free trade zone
d. Competitive

7. _________ is, in very basic words, a position a firm occupies against its competitors.

According to Michael Porter, the three methods for creating a sustainable _________ are through:

1. Cost leadership - Cost advantage occurs when a firm delivers the same services as its competitors but at a lower cost;

2.

a. 180SearchAssistant
b. 6-3-5 Brainwriting
c. Power III
d. Competitive advantage

8. In economics, _________ is the desire to own something and the ability to pay for it. The term _________ signifies the ability or the willingness to buy a particular commodity at a given point of time .

.

a. Discretionary spending
b. Market dominance
c. Demand
d. Market system

9. _________ in economics and business is the result of an exchange and from that trade we assign a numerical monetary value to a good, service or asset. If I trade 4 apples for an orange, the _________ of an orange is 4 - apples. Inversely, the _________ of an apple is 1/4 oranges.

a. Pricing
b. Price
c. Discounts and allowances
d. Contribution margin-based pricing

10. In economics, _________ is the ratio of the percent change in one variable to the percent change in another variable. It is a tool for measuring the responsiveness of a function to changes in parameters in a relative way. Commonly analyzed are _________ of substitution, price and wealth.

a. Intellectual property
b. ACNielsen
c. Opinion leadership
d. Elasticity

11. A _________ is a plan of action designed to achieve a particular goal.

_________ is different from tactics. In military terms, tactics is concerned with the conduct of an engagement while _________ is concerned with how different engagements are linked.

a. Power III
b. 180SearchAssistant
c. 6-3-5 Brainwriting
d. Strategy

12. _________ is the identity of a group or culture, or of an individual as far as one is influenced by one's belonging to a group or culture. _________ is similar to and has overlaps with, but is not synonymous with, identity politics.

There are modern questions of culture that are transferred into questions of identity.

a. Power III
b. 180SearchAssistant
c. 6-3-5 Brainwriting
d. Cultural identity

13. _________ in organizations and public policy is both the organizational process of creating and maintaining a plan; and the psychological process of thinking about the activities required to create a desired goal on some scale. As such, it is a fundamental property of intelligent behavior. This thought process is essential to the creation and refinement of a plan, or integration of it with other plans, that is, it combines forecasting of developments with the preparation of scenarios of how to react to them.

a. 180SearchAssistant
b. 6-3-5 Brainwriting
c. Power III
d. Planning

14. _________s is the social science that studies the production, distribution, and consumption of goods and services. The term _________s comes from the Ancient Greek oá¼°κονομÎ¯α from oá¼¶κος (oikos, 'house') + vÏŒμος (nomos, 'custom' or 'law'), hence 'rules of the house(hold)'. Current _________ models developed out of the broader field of political economy in the late 19th century, owing to a desire to use an empirical approach more akin to the physical sciences.

a. Economic
b. Industrial organization
c. ACNielsen
d. ADTECH

15. _________ are various forms of controls imposed by a government on the purchase/sale of foreign currencies by residents or on the purchase/sale of local currency by nonresidents.

Common _________ include:

- Banning the use of foreign currency within the country
- Banning locals from possessing foreign currency
- Restricting currency exchange to government-approved exchangers
- Fixed exchange rates
- Restrictions on the amount of currency that may be imported or exported

Countries with _________ are also known as 'Article 14 countries,' after the provision in the International Monetary Fund agreement allowing exchange controls for transitional economies. Such controls used to be common in most countries, particularly poorer ones, until the 1990s when free trade and globalization started a trend towards economic liberalization. Today, countries which still impose exchange controls are the exception rather than the rule.

a. 180SearchAssistant
b. 6-3-5 Brainwriting
c. Power III
d. Foreign exchange controls

16. _________ is the state or fact of exclusive rights and control over property, which may be an object, land/real estate, or some other kind of property (like government-granted monopolies collectively referred to as intellectual property.) It is embodied in an _________ right also referred to as title.

_________ is the key building block in the development of the capitalist socio-economic system.

a. ADTECH
b. AMAX
c. ACNielsen
d. Ownership

17. Levi Strauss, born Löb Strauss (February 26, 1829 - September 26, 1902) was a German-Jewish immigrant to the United States who founded the first company to manufacture blue jeans. His firm, _________, began in 1853 in San Francisco, California.

Levi Strauss was born in Bavaria, Germany, to Hirsch Strauss and his wife Rebecca (Haas) Strauss.

a. Albert Einstein
b. AStore
c. African Americans
d. Levi Strauss ' Company

18. A _________ is a process that can allow an organization to concentrate its limited resources on the greatest opportunities to increase sales and achieve a sustainable competitive advantage. A _________ should be centered around the key concept that customer satisfaction is the main goal.

A _________ is most effective when it is an integral component of corporate strategy, defining how the organization will successfully engage customers, prospects, and competitors in the market arena.

a. Cyberdoc
b. Psychographic
c. Societal marketing
d. Marketing strategy

19. The _________ is a trilateral trade bloc in North America created by the governments of the United States, Canada, and Mexico. It superseded the Canada-United States Free Trade Agreement between the US and Canada.

Following diplomatic negotiations dating back to 1990 between the three nations, the leaders met in San Antonio, Texas on December 17, 1992 to sign _________.

a. 180SearchAssistant
b. Power III
c. 6-3-5 Brainwriting
d. North American Free Trade Agreement

20. A _________ is a tax imposed on goods when they are moved across a political boundary. They are usually associated with protectionism, the economic policy of restraining trade between nations. For political reasons, _________s are usually imposed on imported goods, although they may also be imposed on exported goods.

a. Fiscal policy
b. Power III
c. Monetary policy
d. Tariff

21. _________ in its literal sense is the process of transformation of local or regional phenomena into global ones. It can be described as a process by which the people of the world are unified into a single society and function together.

This process is a combination of economic, technological, sociocultural and political forces.

a. 6-3-5 Brainwriting
b. 180SearchAssistant
c. Power III
d. Globalization

22. A _________ is a collection of symbols, experiences and associations connected with a product, a service, a person or any other artifact or entity.

_________s have become increasingly important components of culture and the economy, now being described as 'cultural accessories and personal philosophies'.

Some people distinguish the psychological aspect of a _________ from the experiential aspect.

a. Store brand
b. Brand
c. Brand equity
d. Brandable software

23. Organizational culture is not the same as _________. It is wider and deeper concepts, something that an organization 'is' rather than what it 'has' (according to Buchanan and Huczynski.)

_________ is the total sum of the values, customs, traditions and meanings that make a company unique.

a. Power III
b. 180SearchAssistant
c. Corporate culture
d. Cross-functional team

24. _________ is difficult to define. For example, in 1952, Alfred Kroeber and Clyde Kluckhohn compiled a list of 164 definitions of '_________' in _________: A Critical Review of Concepts and Definitions. However, the word '_________' is most commonly used in three basic senses:

- excellence of taste in the fine arts and humanities
- an integrated pattern of human knowledge, belief, and behavior that depends upon the capacity for symbolic thought and social learning
- the set of shared attitudes, values, goals, and practices that characterizes an institution, organization or group.

When the concept first emerged in eighteenth- and nineteenth-century Europe, it connoted a process of cultivation or improvement, as in agriculture or horticulture. In the nineteenth century, it came to refer first to the betterment or refinement of the individual, especially through education, and then to the fulfillment of national aspirations or ideals.

a. African Americans
b. Albert Einstein
c. AStore
d. Culture

25. _________ is a broad label that refers to any individuals or households that use goods and services generated within the economy. The concept of a _________ is used in different contexts, so that the usage and significance of the term may vary.

A _________ is a person who uses any product or service.

a. 180SearchAssistant
b. Consumer
c. Power III
d. 6-3-5 Brainwriting

26. _________ or _________ data refers to selected population characteristics as used in government, marketing or opinion research, or the _________ profiles used in such research. Note the distinction from the term 'demography' Commonly-used _________ include race, age, income, disabilities, mobility (in terms of travel time to work or number of vehicles available), educational attainment, home ownership, employment status, and even location.

a. AStore
b. Albert Einstein
c. Demographic
d. African Americans

27. Consumer market research is a form of applied sociology that concentrates on understanding the behaviours, whims and preferences, of consumers in a market-based economy, and aims to understand the effects and comparative success of marketing campaigns. The field of consumer _________ as a statistical science was pioneered by Arthur Nielsen with the founding of the ACNielsen Company in 1923 .

Thus _________ is the systematic and objective identification, collection, analysis, and dissemination of information for the purpose of assisting management in decision making related to the identification and solution of problems and opportunities in marketing.

a. Focus group
b. Logit analysis
c. Marketing research process
d. Marketing research

28. _________s are used in open sentences. For instance, in the formula x + 1 = 5, x is a _________ which represents an 'unknown' number. _________s are often represented by letters of the Roman alphabet, or those of other alphabets, such as Greek, and use other special symbols.

a. Variable
b. Book of business
c. Personalization
d. Quantitative

29. _________ refer to a collection of facts usually collected as the result of experience, observation or experiment or a set of premises. This may consist of numbers, words particularly as measurements or observations of a set of variables. _________ are often viewed as a lowest level of abstraction from which information and knowledge are derived.

a. Mean
b. Sample size
c. Pearson product-moment correlation coefficient
d. Data

30. _________ is the ongoing process of identifying and articulating market requirements that define a product's feature set.

a. Product planning
b. Targeted advertising
c. Brand parity
d. Market intelligence

31. _________ is a form of communication that typically attempts to persuade potential customers to purchase or to consume more of a particular brand of product or service. 'While now central to the contemporary global economy and the reproduction of global production networks, it is only quite recently that _________ has been more than a marginal influence on patterns of sales and production. The formation of modern _________ was intimately bound up with the emergence of new forms of monopoly capitalism around the end of the 19th and beginning of the 20th century as one element in corporate strategies to create, organize and where possible control markets, especially for mass produced consumer goods.

a. Advertising
b. ADTECH
c. ACNielsen
d. AMAX

32. A _________ is a type of wholesale merchant business that buys goods and bulk products from importers, other wholesalers and then sells to retailers. _________s can deal in any commodity destined for the retail market. Typical categories are food, lumber, hardware, fuel, and textiles.

a. Jobbing house
b. Refusal to deal
c. Tacit collusion
d. Chief privacy officer

33. _________ is one of the four elements of marketing mix. An organization or set of organizations (go-betweens) involved in the process of making a product or service available for use or consumption by a consumer or business user.

The other three parts of the marketing mix are product, pricing, and promotion.

a. Japan Advertising Photographers' Association
b. Better Living Through Chemistry
c. Distribution
d. Comparison-Shopping agent

34. An _________ is a series of advertisement messages that share a single idea and theme which make up an integrated marketing communication (IMC.) _________s appear in different media across a specific time frame.

The critical part of making an _________ is determining a campaign theme, as it sets the tone for the individual advertisements and other forms of marketing communications that will be used.

a. Advertising campaign
b. ADTECH
c. AMAX
d. ACNielsen

35. Procter is a surname, and may also refer to:

- Bryan Waller Procter (pseud. Barry Cornwall), English poet
- Goodwin Procter, American law firm
- _________, consumer products multinational

.

a. Flyer
b. Convergent
c. Black PRies
d. Procter ' Gamble

36. A _________ is a systematic approach to selling a product or service. A growing body of published literature approaches the _________ from the point of view of an engineering discipline

Reasons for having a well thought-out _________ include seller and buyer risk management, standardized customer interaction in sales, and scalable revenue generation.

a. Sales process
b. Request for proposal
c. Sales management
d. Lead generation

37. _________ is one of the four Ps of the marketing mix. The other three aspects are product, promotion, and place. It is also a key variable in microeconomic price allocation theory.

a. Competitor indexing
b. Price
c. Relationship based pricing
d. Pricing

38. _________ involves disseminating information about a product, product line, brand, or company. It is one of the four key aspects of the marketing mix. (The other three elements are product marketing, pricing, and distribution). P>_________ is generally sub-divided into two parts:

- Above the line _________: Promotion in the media (e.g. TV, radio, newspapers, Internet and Mobile Phones) in which the advertiser pays an advertising agency to place the ad
- Below the line _________: All other _________. Much of this is intended to be subtle enough for the consumer to be unaware that _________ is taking place. E.g. sponsorship, product placement, endorsements, sales _________, merchandising, direct mail, personal selling, public relations, trade shows

a. Davie Brown Index
b. Cashmere Agency
c. Promotion
d. Bottling lines

39. _________ is one of the four aspects of promotional mix. (The other three parts of the promotional mix are advertising, personal selling, and publicity/public relations.) Media and non-media marketing communication are employed for a pre-determined, limited time to increase consumer demand, stimulate market demand or improve product availability.

a. Sales promotion
b. Marketing communication
c. New Media Strategies
d. Merchandise

40. _________ is exchange of capital, goods, and services across international borders or territories. In most countries, it represents a significant share of gross domestic product (GDP.) While _________ has been present throughout much of history , its economic, social, and political importance has been on the rise in recent centuries.

a. ACNielsen
b. International trade
c. Incoterms
d. ADTECH

41. A _________ is an entity formed between two or more parties to undertake economic activity together. The parties agree to create a new entity by both contributing equity, and they then share in the revenues, expenses, and control of the enterprise. The venture can be for one specific project only, or a continuing business relationship such as the Fuji Xerox _________.

a. Joint venture
b. Gripe site
c. Consumer protection
d. Trademark attorney

42. The verb _________ or grant _________ means to give permission. The noun _________ refers to that permission as well as to the document memorializing that permission. _________ may be granted by a party to another party as an element of an agreement between those parties.

a. License
b. Power III
c. 6-3-5 Brainwriting
d. 180SearchAssistant

43. _________ refers to the methods of practicing and using another person's philosophy of business. The franchisor grants the independent operator the right to distribute its products, techniques, and trademarks for a percentage of gross monthly sales and a royalty fee. Various tangibles and intangibles such as national or international advertising, training, and other support services are commonly made available by the franchisor.

a. Power III
b. 180SearchAssistant
c. Franchising
d. Franchise fee

44. The _________ is generally accepted as the use and specification of the four p's describing the strategic position of a product in the marketplace. One version of the origins of the _________ starts in 1948 when James Culliton said that a marketing decision should be a result of something similar to a recipe. This version continued in 1953 when Neil Borden, in his American Marketing Association presidential address, took the recipe idea one step further and coined the term 'Marketing-Mix'.

a. 180SearchAssistant
b. 6-3-5 Brainwriting
c. Marketing mix
d. Power III

45. _________ is a strategic planning method used to evaluate the Strengths, Weaknesses, Opportunities, and Threats involved in a project or in a business venture. It involves specifying the objective of the business venture or project and identifying the internal and external factors that are favorable and unfavorable to achieving that objective. The technique is credited to Albert Humphrey, who led a research project at Stanford University in the 1960s and 1970s using data from Fortune 500 companies.

a. SWOT analysis
b. Lead scoring
c. Market environment
d. Product differentiation

46. An _________ is the manufacturing of a good or service within a category. Although _________ is a broad term for any kind of economic production, in economics and urban planning _________ is a synonym for the secondary sector, which is a type of economic activity involved in the manufacturing of raw materials into goods and products.

There are four key industrial economic sectors: the primary sector, largely raw material extraction industries such as mining and farming; the secondary sector, involving refining, construction, and manufacturing; the tertiary sector, which deals with services (such as law and medicine) and distribution of manufactured goods; and the quaternary sector, a relatively new type of knowledge _________ focusing on technological research, design and development such as computer programming, and biochemistry.

a. ADTECH
b. AMAX
c. ACNielsen
d. Industry

47. _________ is a marketing term, and involves evaluating the situation and trends in a particular company's market. _________ is often called the 'three c's', which refers to the three major elements that must be studied:

- Customers
- Costs
- Competition

The number of 'c's' is sometimes extended to four, five, or even six, with 'Collaboration', 'Company', and 'Competitive advantage'.

- Marketing mix
- SWOT analysis

.

a. Power III
b. 6-3-5 Brainwriting
c. 180SearchAssistant
d. Situation analysis

48. In economics and especially in the theory of competition, _________ are obstacles in the path of a firm that make it difficult to enter a given market.

_________ are the source of a firm's pricing power - the ability of a firm to raise prices without losing all its customers.

The term refers to hindrances that an individual may face while trying to gain entrance into a profession or trade.

a. Barriers to entry
b. Predatory pricing
c. 180SearchAssistant
d. Power III

49. A supply chain is the system of organizations, people, technology, activities, information and resources involved in moving a product or service from _________ to customer. Supply chain activities transform natural resources, raw materials and components into a finished product that is delivered to the end customer. In sophisticated supply chain systems, used products may re-enter the supply chain at any point where residual value is recyclable.

a. Supplier
b. Bringin' Home the Oil
c. Rebate
d. Product line extension

50. _________ is a process of gathering, modeling, and transforming data with the goal of highlighting useful information, suggesting conclusions, and supporting decision making. _________ has multiple facets and approaches, encompassing diverse techniques under a variety of names, in different business, science, and social science domains.

Data mining is a particular _________ technique that focuses on modeling and knowledge discovery for predictive rather than purely descriptive purposes.

a. 180SearchAssistant
b. 6-3-5 Brainwriting
c. Power III
d. Data analysis

51. The break-even point for a product is the point where total revenue received equals the total costs associated with the sale of the product (TR=TC.) A break-even point is typically calculated in order for businesses to determine if it would be profitable to sell a proposed product, as opposed to attempting to modify an existing product instead so it can be made lucrative. _________ can also be used to analyse the potential profitability of an expenditure in a sales-based business.

In _________, margin of safety is how much output or sales level can fall before a business reaches its break-even point (BEP).

a. Break even analysis
b. Contribution margin-based pricing
c. Price skimming
d. Pay Per Sale

52. In economics ' business, specifically cost accounting, the _________ is the point at which cost or expenses and revenue are equal: there is no net loss or gain, and one has 'broken even'. A profit or a loss has not been made, although opportunity costs have been paid, and capital has received the risk-adjusted, expected return.

For example, if the business sells less than 200 tables each month, it will make a loss, if it sells more, it will be a profit.

a. 180SearchAssistant
b. Break-even point
c. Power III
d. Total revenue

53. In cost-volume-profit analysis, a form of management accounting, _________ is the marginal profit per unit sale. It is a useful quantity in carrying out various calculations, and can be used as a measure of operating leverage.

The Total _________ is Total Revenue (TR, or Sales) minus Total Variable Cost (TVC):

TContribution margin = TR - TVC

The Unit _________ (C) is Unit Revenue (Price, P) minus Unit Variable Cost (V):

C = P - V

The _________ Ratio is the percentage of Contribution over Total Revenue, which can be calculated from the unit contribution over unit price or total contribution over Total Revenue:

$$\frac{C}{P} = \frac{P - V}{P} = \frac{\text{Unit Contribution Margin}}{\text{Price}} = \frac{\text{Total Contribution Margin}}{\text{Total Revenue}}$$

For instance, if the price is $10 and the unit variable cost is $2, then the unit _________ is $8, and the _________ ratio is $8/ $10 = 80%.

a. 180SearchAssistant
b. Customer profitability
c. Contribution margin
d. Power III

54. In economics, _________ are business expenses that are not dependent on the activities of the business They tend to be time-related, such as salaries or rents being paid per month. This is in contrast to variable costs, which are volume-related (and are paid per quantity.)

In management accounting, _________ are defined as expenses that do not change in proportion to the activity of a business, within the relevant period or scale of production.

a. Transaction cost
b. Marginal cost
c. Fixed costs
d. Variable cost

55. _________s are expenses that change in proportion to the activity of a business. In other words, _________ is the sum of marginal costs. It can also be considered normal costs.

a. Marginal cost
b. Fixed costs
c. Transaction cost
d. Variable cost

56. In economics, business, retail, and accounting, a _________ is the value of money that has been used up to produce something, and hence is not available for use anymore. In economics, a _________ is an alternative that is given up as a result of a decision. In business, the _________ may be one of acquisition, in which case the amount of money expended to acquire it is counted as _________.

a. Cost
b. Variable cost
c. Transaction cost
d. Fixed costs

57. A personal and cultural _________ is a relative ethic _________, an assumption upon which implementation can be extrapolated. A _________ system is a set of consistent _________s and measures that is soo not true. A principle _________ is a foundation upon which other _________s and measures of integrity are based.

a. Perceptual maps
b. Package-on-Package
c. Supreme Court of the United States
d. Value

58. The _________ is an expected return that the provider of capital plans to earn on their investment.

Capital (money) used for funding a business should earn returns for the capital providers who risk their capital. For an investment to be worthwhile, the expected return on capital must be greater than the _________.

a. Cost of capital
b. Power III
c. 6-3-5 Brainwriting
d. 180SearchAssistant

59.

_________ is a systematic method to improve the 'value' of goods or products and services by using an examination of function. Value, as defined, is the ratio of function to cost. Value can therefore be increased by either improving the function or reducing the cost.

a. Productivity
b. Power III
c. 180SearchAssistant
d. Value engineering

60. In finance, the _________ or quick ratio or liquid ratio measures the ability of a company to use its near cash or quick assets to immediately extinguish or retire its current liabilities. Quick assets include those current assets that presumably can be quickly converted to cash at close to their book values.

$$\text{Quick (Acid Test) Ratio} = \frac{\text{Cash} + \text{Marketable Securities} + \text{Accounts Receivables}}{\text{Current Liabilities}}$$

Generally, the acid test ratio should be 1:1 or better, however this varies widely by industry.

a. ACNielsen
b. AMAX
c. Acid-test
d. ADTECH

61. The _________ is a financial ratio that measures whether or not a firm has enough resources to pay its debts over the next 12 months. It compares a firm's current assets to its current liabilities. It is expressed as follows:

$$\text{Current ratio} = \frac{\text{Current Assets}}{\text{Current Liabilities}}$$

For example, if WXY Company's current assets are $50,000,000 and its current liabilities are $40,000,000, then its _________ would be $50,000,000 divided by $40,000,000, which equals 1.25.

a. 180SearchAssistant
b. Power III
c. 6-3-5 Brainwriting
d. Current ratio

62. The _________ is an independent agency of the United States government, established in 1914 by the _________ Act. Its principal mission is the promotion of 'consumer protection' and the elimination and prevention of what regulators perceive to be harmfully 'anti-competitive' business practices, such as coercive monopoly.

The _________ Act was one of President Wilson's major acts against trusts.

a. 180SearchAssistant
b. Power III
c. 6-3-5 Brainwriting
d. Federal Trade Commission

63. _________ is a list for goods and materials held available in stock by a business. It is also used for a list of the contents of a household and for a list for testamentary purposes of the possessions of someone who has died. In accounting _________ is considered an asset.

a. Ending Inventory
b. ACNielsen
c. ADTECH
d. Inventory

64. The _________ is an equation that equals the cost of goods sold divided by the average inventory. Average inventory equals beginning inventory plus ending inventory divided by 2.

The formula for _________:

$$\text{Inventory Turnover} = \frac{\text{Cost of Goods Sold}}{\text{Average Inventory}}$$

The formula for average inventory:

$$\text{Average Inventory} = \frac{\text{Beginning inventory}+\text{Ending inventory}}{2}$$

A low turnover rate may point to overstocking, obsolescence, or deficiencies in the product line or marketing effort.

a. AMAX b. Inventory turnover
c. ACNielsen d. ADTECH

65. _________ is one of the Accounting Liquidity ratios, a financial ratio. This ratio measures the number of times, on average, the inventory is sold during the period. Its purpose is to measure the liquidity of the inventory.
a. ACNielsen b. ADTECH
c. Internality d. Inventory turnover ratio

66. The U.S. _________ is an independent agency of the United States government which holds primary responsibility for enforcing the federal securities laws and regulating the securities industry, the nation's stock and options exchanges, and other electronic securities markets. The SEC was created by section 4 of the Securities Exchange Act of 1934 (now codified as 15 U.S.C. Â§ 78d and commonly referred to as the 1934 Act.)
a. 6-3-5 Brainwriting b. 180SearchAssistant
c. Power III d. Securities and Exchange Commission

67. _________ is the examining of goods or services from retailers with the intent to purchase at that time. _________ is an activity of selection and/or purchase. In some contexts it is considered a leisure activity as well as an economic one.
a. Khodebshchik b. Hawkers
c. Shopping d. Discount store

68. _________, also referred to as i-marketing, web marketing, online marketing is the marketing of products or services over the Internet.

The Internet has brought many unique benefits to marketing, one of which being lower costs for the distribution of information and media to a global audience. The interactive nature of _________, both in terms of providing instant response and eliciting responses, is a unique quality of the medium.

a. ADTECH b. ACNielsen
c. AMAX d. Internet marketing

69. _________ is an advertisement in which a particular product specifically mentions a competitor by name for the express purpose of showing why the competitor is inferior to the product naming it.

This should not be confused with parody advertisements, where a fictional product is being advertised for the purpose of poking fun at the particular advertisement, nor should it be confused with the use of a coined brand name for the purpose of comparing the product without actually naming an actual competitor. ('Wikipedia tastes better and is less filling than the Encyclopedia Galactica.')

In the 1980s, during what has been referred to as the cola wars, soft-drink manufacturer Pepsi ran a series of advertisements where people, caught on hidden camera, in a blind taste test, chose Pepsi over rival Coca-Cola.

a. Heavy-up
b. GL-70
c. Cost per conversion
d. Comparative advertising

70. _________ can be regarded as an outcome of mental processes (cognitive process) leading to the selection of a course of action among several alternatives. Every _________ process produces a final choice. The output can be an action or an opinion of choice.

a. 180SearchAssistant
b. Power III
c. 6-3-5 Brainwriting
d. Decision making

71. _________ is systematic determination of merit, worth, and significance of something or someone using criteria against a set of standards. _________ often is used to characterize and appraise subjects of interest in a wide range of human enterprises, including the arts, criminal justice, foundations and non-profit organizations, government, health care, and other human services.

Depending on the topic of interest, there are professional groups which look to the quality and rigor of the _________ process.

a. Evaluation
b. ACNielsen
c. AMAX
d. ADTECH

72. _________ refers to the marketing effects or outcomes that accrue to a product with its brand name compared with those that would accrue if the same product did not have the brand name . And, at the root of these marketing effects is consumers' knowledge. In other words, consumers' knowledge about a brand makes manufacturers/advertisers respond differently or adopt appropriately adapt measures for the marketing of the brand .

a. Brand equity
b. Brand image
c. Product extension
d. Brand aversion

73. _________ is the term given to food that can be prepared and served very quickly. While any meal with low preparation time can be considered to be _________, typically the term refers to food sold in a restaurant or store with low quality preparation and served to the customer in a packaged form for take-out/take-away. The term '_________' was recognized in a dictionary by Merriam-Webster in 1951.

a. Fast Food
b. 6-3-5 Brainwriting
c. Power III
d. 180SearchAssistant

74. _________ , according to The American Marketing Association, is 'a planning process designed to assure that all brand contacts received by a customer or prospect for a product, service, or organization are relevant to that person and consistent over time.' (Marketing Power Dictionary)

_________ is a term used to describe a holistic approach to marketing. It aims to ensure consistency of message and the complementary use of media. The concept includes online and offline marketing channels.

a. ADTECH
b. Integrated marketing communications
c. AMAX
d. ACNielsen

75. _________ refers to messages and related media used to communicate with a market. Those who practice advertising, branding, direct marketing, graphic design, marketing, packaging, promotion, publicity, sponsorship, public relations, sales, sales promotion and online marketing are termed marketing communicators, _________ managers, or more briefly as marcom managers.

a. Sales promotion
b. Merchandising
c. Merchandise
d. Marketing communication

76. A _________ strategy targets non-buying customers in currently targeted segments. It also targets new customers in new segments. (Winer)

A marketing manager has to think about the following questions before implementing a _________ strategy: Is it profitable? Will it require the introduction of new or modified products? Is the customer and channel well enough researched and understood?

The marketing manager uses these four groups to give more focus to the market segment decision: existing customers, competitor customers, non-buying in current segments, new segments.

a. Commercial planning
b. Market development
c. Perceptual mapping
d. Kano model

77. In business and engineering, new _________ is the term used to describe the complete process of bringing a new product or service to market. There are two parallel paths involved in the Nproduct development process: one involves the idea generation, product design, and detail engineering; the other involves market research and marketing analysis. Companies typically see new _________ as the first stage in generating and commercializing new products within the overall strategic process of product life cycle management used to maintain or grow their market share.

a. New product screening
b. Specification tree
c. Product development
d. New product development

78. A _________ is a type of department store, which sell products at prices lower than those asked by traditional retail outlets. Most discount department stores offer wide assortments of goods; others specialize in such merchandise as jewelry, electronic equipment, or electrical appliances. _________s are not dollar stores, which sell goods at a dollar or less.

a. Discount store
b. Sales per unit area
c. Strip mall
d. Gruen transfer

79. In economics, a _________ is a good for which demand increases more than proportionally as income rises, in contrast to a 'necessity good', for which demand increases less than proportionally as income rises.

_________s are said to have high income elasticity of demand: as people become wealthier, they will buy more and more of the _________. This also means, however, that should there be a decline in income its demand will drop.

a. Luxury good
b. Power III
c. Durable good
d. Free good

80. The term _________ is used to describe a nation's social or business activity in the process of rapid growth and industrialization. Currently, there are approximately 28 _________ in the world, with the economies of China and India considered to be two of the largest. According to The Economist many people find the term dated, but a new term has yet to gain much traction.

a. Outsourcing
b. In-house
c. ACNielsen
d. Emerging markets

81. _________ is a form of government regulation which protects the interests of consumers. For example, a government may require businesses to disclose detailed information about products--particularly in areas where safety or public health is an issue, such as food. _________ is linked to the idea of consumer rights (that consumers have various rights as consumers), and to the formation of consumer organizations which help consumers make better choices in the marketplace.

a. Trademark dilution
b. Federal Bureau of Investigation
c. Consumer Protection
d. Sound trademark

82. A _________ product is an imitation which infringes upon a production monopoly held by either a state or corporation. Goods are produced with the intent to bypass this monopoly and thus take advantage of the established worth of the previous product. The word _________ frequently describes both the forgeries of currency and documents, as well as the imitations of clothing, software, pharmaceuticals, watches, electronics, and company logos and brands.

a. 180SearchAssistant
b. 6-3-5 Brainwriting
c. Power III
d. Counterfeit

83. _________ refers to 'controlling human or societal behaviour by rules or restrictions.' _________ can take many forms: legal restrictions promulgated by a government authority, self-_________, social _________, co-_________ and market _________. One can consider _________ as actions of conduct imposing sanctions (such as a fine.) This action of administrative law, or implementing regulatory law, may be contrasted with statutory or case law.

a. Rule of four
b. Regulation
c. CAN-SPAM
d. Non-conventional trademark

84. In marketing, _________ has come to mean the process by which marketers try to create an image or identity in the minds of their target market for its product, brand, or organization. It is the 'relative competitive comparison' their product occupies in a given market as perceived by the target market.

Re-_________ involves changing the identity of a product, relative to the identity of competing products, in the collective minds of the target market.

a. Positioning
b. GE matrix
c. Containerization
d. Moratorium

85. _________ is the provision of service to customers before, during and after a purchase.

According to Turban et al., '_________ is a series of activities designed to enhance the level of customer satisfaction - that is, the feeling that a product or service has met the customer expectation.'

Its importance varies by product, industry and customer.

a. COPC Inc.
b. Customer service
c. Customer experience
d. Facing

86. _________ is an American magazine published monthly by Consumers Union. It publishes reviews and comparisons of consumer products and services based on reporting and results from its in-house testing laboratory. It also publishes cleaning and general buying guides.

a. Consumer Reports
b. Crossing the Chasm
c. Power III
d. Magalog

87. A _________ is a retail establishment which specializes in selling a wide range of products without a single predominant merchandise line. _________s usually sell products including apparel, furniture, appliances, electronics, and additionally select other lines of products such as paint, hardware, toiletries, cosmetics, photographic equipment, jewelery, toys, and sporting goods. Certain _________s are further classified as discount _________s.

a. 180SearchAssistant
b. 6-3-5 Brainwriting
c. Power III
d. Department store

88. In finance, an _________ is a contract between a buyer and a seller that gives the buyer the right--but not the obligation--to buy or to sell a particular asset (the underlying asset) at a later day at an agreed price. In return for granting the _________, the seller collects a payment (the premium) from the buyer. A call _________ gives the buyer the right to buy the underlying asset; a put _________ gives the buyer of the _________ the right to sell the underlying asset.

a. ADTECH
b. AMAX
c. ACNielsen
d. Option

89. The loyalty business model is a business model used in strategic management in which company resources are employed so as to increase the loyalty of customers and other stakeholders in the expectation that corporate objectives will be met or surpassed. A typical example of this type of model is: quality of product or service leads to customer satisfaction, which leads to _________, which leads to profitability.

Fredrick Reichheld (1996) expanded the loyalty business model beyond customers and employees.

a. Customer loyalty
b. Power III
c. 6-3-5 Brainwriting
d. 180SearchAssistant

Chapter 1

1. d	2. b	3. d	4. a	5. d	6. d	7. b	8. c	9. a	10. d
11. a	12. a	13. d	14. d	15. a	16. b	17. d	18. b	19. b	20. a
21. c	22. a	23. d	24. b	25. d	26. c	27. d	28. d	29. b	30. c
31. a	32. d	33. d	34. d	35. b	36. a	37. b	38. b	39. d	40. a
41. d	42. d	43. a	44. d	45. d	46. a	47. d	48. d		

Chapter 2

1. d	2. d	3. d	4. b	5. d	6. d	7. a	8. b	9. d	10. a
11. b	12. b	13. b	14. d	15. c	16. c	17. c	18. c	19. a	20. b
21. d	22. d	23. b	24. c	25. a	26. a	27. a	28. c	29. d	30. a
31. d	32. b	33. b	34. b	35. d	36. d	37. d	38. a		

Chapter 3

1. b	2. d	3. a	4. a	5. d	6. c	7. d	8. d	9. c	10. c
11. d	12. d	13. b	14. b	15. d	16. a	17. c	18. d	19. c	20. c
21. c	22. d	23. a	24. a	25. b	26. c	27. d	28. c	29. d	30. d

Chapter 4

1. a	2. d	3. d	4. d	5. b	6. c	7. d	8. d	9. c	10. b
11. d	12. d	13. c	14. d	15. a	16. d	17. c	18. d	19. b	20. b
21. a	22. a	23. d	24. d						

Chapter 5

1. d	2. d	3. a	4. b	5. a	6. d	7. d	8. d	9. b	10. a
11. c	12. d	13. d	14. b	15. a	16. d	17. d	18. d		

Chapter 6

1. d	2. d	3. b	4. c	5. d	6. d	7. d	8. b	9. a	10. b
11. d	12. d	13. d	14. b	15. d	16. d	17. d	18. c	19. d	20. d
21. d	22. d	23. d	24. d	25. a	26. b	27. b	28. d	29. a	30. b
31. a	32. d	33. b	34. a	35. d	36. d	37. c	38. d	39. d	40. d
41. b	42. c	43. b	44. d	45. a	46. b	47. d	48. d	49. c	50. c

Chapter 7

1. b	2. c	3. b	4. a	5. a	6. d	7. d	8. b	9. d	10. a
11. d	12. d	13. d	14. a	15. a	16. a	17. c	18. d	19. d	20. a
21. b	22. b	23. d	24. d	25. d	26. c	27. d	28. c	29. c	30. d
31. d	32. d	33. c	34. a	35. d	36. d	37. d	38. d	39. d	40. d

Chapter 8

1. b	2. b	3. d	4. c	5. c	6. d	7. d	8. d	9. d	10. c
11. d	12. c	13. c	14. b	15. b	16. d	17. d	18. c	19. c	20. d
21. a	22. c	23. d	24. a	25. d	26. d	27. d	28. b	29. a	30. d
31. c	32. d	33. d	34. d	35. c	36. b	37. b	38. b	39. d	40. a
41. d	42. c	43. d	44. d	45. a	46. d				

Chapter 9

1. d	2. d	3. d	4. d	5. c	6. c	7. a	8. b	9. d	10. d
11. c	12. b	13. d	14. c	15. d	16. a	17. d	18. d	19. d	20. d
21. b	22. b	23. d	24. d	25. a	26. d	27. d	28. d	29. d	30. c

Chapter 10

1. a	2. a	3. c	4. b	5. d	6. d	7. c	8. b	9. b	10. d
11. d	12. d	13. b	14. d	15. a	16. d	17. a	18. d	19. a	20. b
21. c	22. b	23. d	24. b	25. d	26. b	27. d	28. a	29. d	30. d
31. d	32. b	33. c	34. a	35. b	36. c	37. c	38. d	39. b	40. d
41. c	42. d	43. d							

Chapter 11

1. a	2. b	3. d	4. d	5. d	6. b	7. d	8. b	9. d	10. d
11. c	12. c	13. c	14. d	15. d	16. d	17. d	18. d	19. c	20. d
21. d	22. d	23. d	24. d	25. c	26. d	27. d	28. c	29. d	30. d
31. c	32. a	33. b	34. d	35. d	36. d	37. b	38. d	39. a	40. b
41. d	42. d	43. d							

Chapter 12

1. c	2. d	3. a	4. d	5. a	6. d	7. d	8. d	9. d	10. d
11. b	12. d	13. c	14. c	15. c	16. d	17. c	18. b	19. c	20. d
21. b	22. a	23. c	24. d	25. d	26. d	27. d	28. c	29. d	30. d
31. d	32. d	33. d	34. b	35. d					

Chapter 13

1. d	2. d	3. d	4. d	5. b	6. d	7. d	8. c	9. b	10. d
11. d	12. d	13. d	14. a	15. d	16. d	17. d	18. d	19. d	20. d
21. d	22. b	23. c	24. d	25. b	26. c	27. d	28. a	29. d	30. a
31. a	32. a	33. c	34. a	35. d	36. a	37. d	38. c	39. a	40. b
41. a	42. a	43. c	44. c	45. a	46. d	47. d	48. a	49. a	50. d
51. a	52. b	53. c	54. c	55. d	56. a	57. d	58. a	59. d	60. c
61. d	62. d	63. d	64. b	65. d	66. d	67. c	68. d	69. d	70. d
71. a	72. a	73. a	74. b	75. d	76. b	77. c	78. a	79. a	80. d
81. c	82. d	83. b	84. a	85. b	86. a	87. d	88. d	89. a	

www.ingramcontent.com/pod-product-compliance
Lightning Source LLC
Chambersburg PA
CBHW082051230426
43670CB00016B/2854
* 9 7 8 1 4 2 8 8 7 3 5 6 8 *